Leaving the Office Behind

Leaving the Office Behind

Dr. Barbara Mackoff

G. P. PUTNAM'S SONS / New York

The author gratefully acknowledges permission from
Chappell & Co., Inc., to quote from "It's My Party,"
copyright © 1963 by Arch Music Co., Inc.
All rights controlled by Chappell & Co., Inc.
International copyright secured. All rights reserved.

Designed by Giorgetta Bell McRee

LIBRARY OF CONGRESS CATALOGING IN PUBLICATION DATA

Mackoff, Barbara.
    Leaving the office behind.

    1. Stress (Psychology) 2. Work—Psychological
aspects. 3. Interpersonal relations. 4. Family.
I. Title.
BF575.S75M23 1984   158   84-12088
ISBN 0-399-12971-5

Printed in the United States of America

Acknowledgments

I am grateful to family, friends and colleagues whose warmth and wisdom helped me to bring this book to completion: Sam and Selma Mackoff, Dan and Natalie Miller, Valerie Coyne, Cora Mackoff, Mavis and John Brodey, Daniel Ramras, Virgil Graham, Ralph Pascualy, Michelle Hasson, Kathleen Nelson and Nancy Sternoff.

Special thanks to my editor and publisher, Phyllis Grann, for her valuable suggestions and continued enthusiastic response, Stacy Creamer whose editing added clarity and sparkle, Jane Adams for her marvelous advice, and to a very special agent, Amy Berkower, who shared my excitement about the book and provided gracious and knowledgeable support.

My appreciation to Darlene Cox, Jodie Eveland and Taffy Evans, who worked with grace under pressure in the preparation of the manuscript.

I want to gratefully acknowledge those of you who talked to me about your lives at work and at home. Your experiences are the heart of this book.

And thank you, Jeremy, for your generosity, your insight and for the pleasure of your company after work

To Jeremy

Contents

Introduction

Turning In Your Suit

I was listening to my father-in-law Dan, a retired chief executive, talk to Ned, also a former executive. They were reminiscing about the cast of characters in the Fortune 500 corporation they had managed in the 1970s.

"What about Mitchell?" Ned asked. "When did he *turn in his suit?*"

I smiled at Ned's use of this picturesque expression for retirement. Then I thought: Most of us don't want to wait forty years to turn in our suits; we want to "retire" at the end of each working day.

And most people—whether they work in a lab coat or a tweed jacket—change clothes immediately when they come home from work. They see the change as a first attempt to leave the day behind.

"When I change my clothes," an attorney explains, "I feel like I am shedding the day, getting back to basics."

As you slip into something more comfortable, you begin the process of softening and transforming the professional image you project on the job. "Turning in your suit" becomes the first ritual

11

in the process of shedding the pressures and accumulated tensions of your day at work.

The theme of the vanishing suit bombards us in its endless media variations; we are amused by men and women who accomplish the transitions between work and home and love with just a rustle of silk or a whiff of perfume.

In this book, I'll take a different position: I believe that coming home from work may be the hardest part of your job. Leaving work behind is not as easy as changing your clothes or changing your perfume.

"SOMETHING ELSE"

She is one of those women who preside over perfume commercials. A lovely woman dressed in a gray flannel suit/pearls/pumps. She is obviously a powerful woman; we know this because the three men at the table are listening intently to her.

The narrator almost whispers his comment: "Chimere, from a distance it is *discreet, elegant.*"

The camera then cuts to another scene with the same woman. She appears, sans suit and bare-shouldered, enjoying some tiny kisses on her neck from a man who was definitely *not* at the business lunch!

Now the punch line: "But up close, Chimere is *something else.*"

In its own silly way, the ad plays on our rich fantasies about coming home from work. It celebrates the distant and discreet cool we project in our professional relationships, and reminds us of how we all hope to be "something else" with the people we meet after work.

Unfortunately, the "something else" that we become at the end of the day is not nearly so delightful as those tiny kisses might suggest.

Coming home from work in our cars and on buses and trains, we all struggle to unwind. We may be exhausted, preoccupied with unfinished projects and unpaid overhead. We may be elated and untouchable, absorbed in our successes and career plans.

Coming home can be a time of abrupt changes, irritability and mismatched rhythms with family and friends.

My husband, Jeremy, is an architect who comes home talking about the downtown development plan, a house in Alaska, a bank on Mercer Island, or a restaurant in Idaho. He sits at dinner preoccupied with design problems or with a client's mercurial moods.

Once I asked him expectantly: "What are you thinking?" He responded, "I'm trying to figure out how to frame the windows on that condominium project."

As a psychotherapist and consultant, I come home thinking about my therapy practice, communication training for the city and stress reduction for bankers. When I shift my attention from myself and my work to my love and interest in Jeremy, I am traveling a great distance. Like most of you, our transition between the demands of work and the relaxation of home and love is not always a graceful passage.

I have had a growing concern about the quality of time that all of us spend at work and at home. My contacts with hundreds of working men and women have convinced me that it is not the pressures of the job that cause us to accumulate stress. Instead, I think it is our inability to leave the pressures behind. The job stress we carry home finds expression in headaches, sexual indifference, cross words and shortened marriages.

This book rests on my belief that the ability to move gracefully between work and home is the prerequisite for creating a balanced life.

Have you been expecting your family and friends to understand your pressures? You may not see the risk of passing on your daily frustrations to the people you love; maybe you think you have an infinite number of chances to learn in order to relax with them.

I want to talk to you out of that position. I am convinced that the pattern of unloading daily stresses on friends and family bears an enormous risk. It is possible to use up the patience and concern of close friends. Sympathy can turn to resentment; empathy can become indifference.

If you carry work home and withhold your laughter and joy, your relationships will change drastically over a short period of time. When this happens, you will have extended your stresses into an even larger territory in your life. You will risk being overwhelmed by stress at work and in love with no relief.

Whether you are single or living with someone, you need to think about techniques you can use to leave work behind and to enjoy the comforts of home and love.

WHY THIS BOOK MAY NOT BE FOR YOU

If your idea of "something else" means changing from your work clothes into a pair of jeans so that you can spend the evening barricaded in your study, this book is not for you.

If you are looking for techniques you can use to persuade your family and friends to understand the enormous amounts of work you bring home, this book is not for you.

This is not a book that will tell you about how to have it all. I won't be alternating information about career development with instructions for sexual acrobatics. You won't find a blueprint for balancing a fantastic career with loving friends, romantic lovers, sparkling homes and problem-free children. I don't believe you *can* have it all.

My focus here is on the quality of the time you spend away from work. My concern is in helping each of you fashion your own style of ending the day and becoming "something else." This is a book about how to come home from work.

SOME TOUGH QUESTIONS

Have you read the study that showed that working people treated complete strangers with more politeness and interest than members of their own family? Before you shrug this off, let me ask you some tough questions.

- Do you spend most of your evenings with family and friends complaining or bragging about work?
- Do you find yourself thinking, "Great, I can go home and really be myself"? (*Translation*: grouchy, unshaven.)

- Do your boss, your clients and co-workers see the best of you and your family and friends see the worst?
- Have you postponed or rescheduled a trip alone with him/her at least two times because of work?
- Do you think that your pressures at work are *just about* to settle down?
- Do you believe "I'll only be in night school for six months. I know that he/she will understand when I am too tired to make love"?

If you answered yes to more than one of these questions, you are probably holding some cherished but dangerous beliefs about your loving relationships outside of work.

THREE CHERISHED BUT DANGEROUS BELIEFS

I want to tamper with your beliefs for a moment. There are three ideas that we all repeat to one another. These cherished beliefs are dangerous to your health because they detract from the strength and richness of your life at home.

You cannot benefit from the approaches in this book unless you are willing to banish these ideas and substitute beliefs that will enrich your life at home and allow you to recover from the stresses of the day.

Belief #1:
"My Family and Friends Will Understand"

I can't stand to read a book that bears the dedication "To Janet, who put up with all of my rages and binges while writing this book."

We all know what this dedication really means. It means the author spent Thanksgiving Day slumped over a bottle of correction fluid. He is talking about his dark mood when the second chapter wasn't falling into place. He is thinking of the times he was preoccupied, with a head full of ideas, and no thought of making love with his long-suffering Janet.

You may be giving yourself the same kind of license for self-absorption. The stress of deadlines and the uncertainties about your job may be causing you to focus only on yourself. Your world is shrinking; you are losing the capacity to consider the needs of the people you love.

This book rests on my belief that your family and friends cannot be expected to endure your rages and binges. Your relationships will starve on a diet of self-absorption. Instead, you need to cultivate your emotional generosity and an ability to respond to the needs of others at the end of the day.

Later I will suggest the kinds of techniques that can help you look outside of yourself. These techniques allow you to put your work aside so your family and friends won't need to duck for cover when you walk through the door.

Belief #2:
"At Home, I Can Really Be Myself"

We all have said it: "I have to impress people all week. I don't want to have to try *that* hard at home."

This is the most cherished and most dangerous belief. You *do* have to impress the people you love. You need to impress them with your love and your interest in them.

There is a difference between being on edge and being attentive. You won't be taking notes during your dinner with a friend. But your family and friends are entitled to your full attention during a conversation. Even if you talk all day, you can't expect a golden silence every evening.

There is a difference between being comfortable and being slovenly. Hot dogs and chili do not require a tie at the dinner table. But consider the possibility of a shave and a shower.

There is a difference between being relaxed and being self-indulgent. You have to choose your words carefully at home, too. If you have saved up an eight-hour nightmare of a day, don't expect three hours of dinner and dessert to tell it to a rapt audience.

Consider an alternative belief: Simple courtesies and self-control are a critical part of all of your important relationships. There are enormous risks in taking rude liberties with the people who love you.

In the chapters that follow you'll find techniques that you can use to recharge your energies at the day's end. These techniques allow you to "be yourself" at home. You will be your most responsive, relaxed and playful self.

Belief #3:
"This Is Only Temporary"

This is pure myth. You lost a big account. Your boss is going through a divorce and counting on you. Collections are terrible. You just have to finish this one big project. You will only be tense until after you see your performance review. You will be able to vacation after you have proved yourself, after you attract one more client or after . . .

The list of detours is endless. You may have told your family and friends: "After this big push, *then* we can dance, sing, sail and make love."

By the time you are available, you may have set up a pattern of hurt and distance that will accompany you long after the "temporary" hard times have ended. Suddenly, you will find that your recent history with family and friends is a backlog of silent, unholy nights.

This book underlines the belief that it is your responsibility to shape yourself into a responsive person at the end of each workday. Your commitment to the important people in your life includes your willingness to stay in continuous loving contact with them.

The techniques that I outline can help you to reduce your feelings of tension and unfinished business and to generate the energy you need to enjoy life away from work.

CONTINUE READING

If you are willing to discard these three beliefs, continue reading. You will find over one hundred suggestions to add grace and delight to the end of your day.

I use techniques and examples from literature, music, politics and movies to offer humorous counterpoint to interviews and case material drawn from my practice as a therapist and consultant. You will encounter characters like Lady Macbeth, Mozart, Nancy Reagan and Humphrey Bogart—each illuminating the difficulties involved in coming home from work.

You will not be able to use all of the techniques with equal comfort or confidence. But remember, you are trying to discard cherished beliefs and change deeply ingrained behavior patterns.

My purpose is to stimulate you to try some different behavior patterns, and many of the techniques are designed to activate the empathic and playful parts of yourself that are dormant during the workday.

The idea is to consider many different approaches to the problems of transition. Your rite of passage should be tailored to your unique personality and to your special relationships with family and friends.

Let's begin by talking about the journey that you will make five times this week.

You will leave work to come home.

Part
ONE

COMING
HOME

Chapter 1

"There Is No Place Like Home"

THE RUBY SLIPPERS

When Dorothy clicked the heels of her ruby slippers in *The Wizard of Oz*, she made the most magical transition between work and home in the history of film.

All she had to do to get from Oz to Kansas was to click those heels and murmur, "There's no place like home, there's no place like home." She awakened to find herself surrounded by Auntie Em and crew.

If we thought of Dorothy as a team manager, we'd have to admit that she had accomplished all of her objectives on that trip to the Emerald City: a heart for the Tin Man, a brain for the Scarecrow, and courage for the Cowardly Lion. She had put in a good week's work.

Dorothy had no trouble leaving Oz. But for most of us, whether we have been off to see the wizard or to *be* the wizard, our transition from work is something less than magical. It takes

much more than a click of our wing tips—or our power pumps—
to ensure a smooth voyage.

You may truly believe that there is no place like home. Yet
you find yourself spending your time there distracted and self-
absorbed. As one accountant puts it, "I spend all day at work and
all evening *thinking* about my work. And I'm not getting paid
overtime!"

Coming home requires that you slow your pace and change
your self-directed focus so that you can encounter friends and
family in a relaxed, responsive mood.

But here is the paradox: In order to leave work behind and
look *outside* of yourself, you need to take one last look *inside*.
This parting focus on yourself will allow you to cast off the pressures of your job and open up the evening for pleasure.

You can begin by postponing the unfinished tasks of the day.

UNFINISHED SYMPHONIES

I have often wondered about Mozart at the end of a difficult day.
Unable to resolve the horn section in his latest opus, he was
terrible company at dinner that evening, probably. How difficult to come home from work with an unfinished symphony on
your mind!

Yet as you leave the office each day, you attempt to leave
behind a similar kind of unfinished business. Check your briefcase. I'll bet that you are bringing home much more than a few
papers.

You probably feel pursued by the phone calls you didn't return. Maybe you are working under a deadline. Your boss wants
to see you tomorrow afternoon and you don't know why. You
need a new idea to present to a client and your mind is completely blank.

Now consider this simple fact: Most unfinished business cannot be finished at home. Why deny yourself an evening of rest
and recuperation? Instead of working "overtime," accomplishing
nothing, why not dance on your kitchen floor, and return to
work feeling refreshed?

If you really plan to come home from work, you need to find ways to postpone the completion of your own unfinished symphonies.

My dear friend, analyst Leonard Mandel, used to call this "postponing anxiety." You can do this with four techniques that allow you to leave unfinished business on your desk.

TECHNIQUE: Listing

As five o'clock draws near, you may be facing the next day with a vague sense of dread. If you feel overwhelmed by the tasks to be finished try to dissolve the dread by translating your free-floating anxiety into specific goals.

List all of the tasks you need to do the next day. Create categories appropriate to your job and list each task under the appropriate category. Then look at your list. Are there any tasks that can be delegated? Any that can be handled later in the week? Finally, assign a priority to each task and a preferred time of day to tackle it.

TECHNIQUE: Seeing and Believing

With list in hand, you can visualize a way to leave your unfinished work behind. Go over each individual item on your list. After you read each item, close your eyes and imagine yourself finishing that task.

Your list may include making a sales presentation to a client or tackling a mound of paperwork. See yourself shaking hands with an interested client after your presentation; picture yourself coming to the bottom of your in-basket.

Consider every item on the list. Visualize the best possible outcome: you were awarded the contract, you completed the report, your students followed all of your instructions.

You can end your day with a picture of yourself completing tomorrow's work. This kind of relief from unfinished business can be a powerful tool in your successful passage from work to home.

But some of the items on your list are problems that require a creative solution. You may not be able to picture the solution and this keeps the problem on your mind. If this is the case, try the next technique.

TECHNIQUE: Delegate to Your Unconscious Mind

You may think that problems at work can be solved only with the focused attention of your conscious mind. When you are pursued by a problem at work, you will have difficulty enjoying your hours at home. Your mind will drift back to the problem you left on your desk; your family will find you aloof and preoccupied.

Think for a moment. How many times have you left a thorny problem with the intention of "sleeping on it," only to wake up with a solution? The next time you feel fresh out of ideas, why not delegate the assignment to your unconscious mind?

To employ this technique, remind yourself that you have spent several days or hours of deliberate thought about the problem and that you don't have any new solutions. Then decide to delegate: "As I relax this evening and sleep tonight, I am going to turn this problem over to my unconscious resources. In the morning (or by 4 P.M. tomorrow) I can expect some fresh ideas on the subject."

This technique can work only if you believe in the power of these resources. Expect to get wild hunches in the shower, new ideas when you are jogging, and creative solutions while you are brushing your teeth, and you will.

If all of these techniques fail, and you are still brooding about unfinished business, take a lesson from Lady Macbeth.

TECHNIQUE: "Out, Damned Spot!"

In the last act of Shakespeare's *Macbeth*, we learn that Lady Macbeth still hasn't recovered from working the night shift.

We find her sleepwalking, going through the motions of washing her hands. She is muttering, "Out, damned spot!" as she attempts to cleanse her thoughts of the night's bloody work.

I hope that your daily tasks are considerably less haunting than murdering a royal relative. But still, you can see that this distressed lady was trying, without success, to use a technique that you can learn right now.

It is called *thought stopping*, and the famous phrase "Out, damned spot!" is the perfect command to interrupt the thoughts about work that you can't wash out of your mind.

Consider Steven's situation. His job involves giving monthly reports to the senior management team in a large organization. For days before his presentation, Steven would be haunted with doubts: Will I stammer? Have I picked out the best slides? What if they don't laugh at my opening joke? Afterward, Steven would engage in a detailed review of his performance.

When you are preoccupied with similar fears, try saying loudly, "Stop!" This command interrupts your negative review of the day or preview of the future and offers the opportunity to redirect your thinking.

If, like Steven, you are worried about choosing the perfect opening line for your talk, try substituting a more positive scenario. Interrupt the flow of negative thoughts by imagining a group of smiling faces around the conference table.

With practice, you can postpone your unfinished business and enjoy your evenings at home. That is, if you can shift into a slower gear, that is.

THE FAST LANE

Coming home involves the process of slowing down. Often the most difficult part of ending the day is shifting from the fast, demanding pace of work to the more relaxed rhythms at home.

Denise, a successful attorney, explains the problem. "I discovered I was applying the same discipline and organization at work and at home. Every *minute* of our vacation was planned and scheduled.

I realized that I needed to stop applying the same intensity to every event in my life. I finally asked myself, what is the worse thing that could happen? The answer: We'd have cold cereal tomorrow."

The fast, intense pace that is habitual at work will block your transition to a relaxing time with family and friends. Here are two approaches that will help you to slow your pace on the way home from work.

TECHNIQUE: Slowing Down

At 4:15 you may find yourself doing your most demanding work. When your day ends with a feverish finale, you probably will carry that intensity with you all the way home. Instead, why not schedule the least demanding tasks for your last hour in the office?

Diane, a city planner, stays an extra half hour after work to unwind. She listens to soothing music on her Sony Walkman, writes in her journal and consults her next day's schedule.

Plan to end your day with your easiest, least pressured tasks. For example, try to use the last thirty minutes to return phone calls, read professional literature, use the copy machine, proofread letters, organize your drawers or clean the top of your desk.

In this way, you will be able to change the focus from your task-oriented day and be available for a relaxed and spontaneous evening.

TECHNIQUE: Postcards from Tahiti

I once saw a picture frame that introduced me to a new technique for slowing down. The edge of the frame was painted with palm trees, blue sky and a sandy beach. The inside of the frame was empty, except for the words "Picture Yourself Here."

Use your imagination to paint yourself inside of that frame. Take a round trip from your stuffy office to Tahiti.

This technique is called *visualization* and can be accomplished by sitting comfortably in your chair and closing your eyes. Pick a favorite spot to visit. You don't have to go to the beach if scaling Mount Washington is your idea of relaxation. Just select a spot where you can slow down.

Did you pick the beach? Begin by picturing yourself walking on the sand toward an expanse of shimmering water. As you settle under a palm frond for the afternoon, take in the smells and the sounds of the ocean: the fresh salty breeze, the foamy bubbles washing ashore. Feel the sun warming your face and hands. You are yawning and stretching lazily, maybe drifting into a nap.

When you feel ready to leave this island retreat, picture yourself walking slowly away from the beach. When you open your eyes, you will notice that your tension has begun to evaporate.

Practice visiting your favorite vacation spot on your way home from work. Even if you can only stay for five minutes, your brief vacation will allow you to feel rested and refreshed. In your relaxed state, you will find it easier to forget about the problems and people you have encountered during the day.

UNINVITED GUESTS

Guess who's coming to dinner? Your boss Ed, who keeps reminding you that you are expendable; Dana, your assistant who rolls her eyes every time you ask her to type a letter; and Ralph, who stops by your desk with a daily report on his embattled marriage.

You say you don't like the guest list? But how many times have you brought these annoying people home with you?

I remember that I spent many candlelight dinners during the early months of my marriage dramatizing every act of a power struggle taking place at the college where I worked. Jeremy and I could have shared our dinner talking about his day, the world at large, or by making silly, sexy plans. Instead, I brought the dean and most of the faculty home for months before I decided to resign.

We can only make the transition from work to love if we leave these unwelcome guests behind.

Work is a contact spot, and each day brings encounters with difficult or disturbing people. The difficult people will vary according to your job description. If your job has a strong element of public contact, you may encounter angry people and unpredictable clients, students and customers. If you are a manager, you may be plagued with uncooperative employees or unsympathetic supervisors.

Many public-sector employees and health practitioners work with people who touch them with a deep sense of sadness. One pediatric nurse had to change her assignment because she was spending her evenings in despair about the beautiful and terminally ill children in her section of the hospital.

Because of your intense encounters with people, you may be coming home with uninvited guests for dinner. Later I will focus on the process of talking to family and friends about work. But for now, let's talk about how to create some distance from the close encounters of the day.

The easiest way to do this is to take one last look at the people in your day before you walk through the front door. Each of the three techniques in this section creates an opportunity to do so and to make a connection with your feelings about these encounters.

Your day moved so swiftly that you may be unaware of the unexpressed feelings about the people that you have been bringing home to dinner. These difficult encounters and unspoken feelings may have left you in a funk that you can't explain.

If you are unaware of your feelings, you will have difficulty in leaving the day behind. Your family may spend the evening playing that unpopular parlor game "What's wrong with Daddy (or Mommy) tonight?"

Each of the ideas in this section assumes your responsibility in spending time to discover how your day has affected you. This is a vital aspect of coming home from work.

Here are the techniques that can help you break the habit of setting extra places at your dinner table.

TECHNIQUE: Roll the Credits

Borrow this technique from the movies. In most films, the cast of characters runs at the end of the movie. This signals the end of the movie and helps the audience review who danced and kissed and died during the last ninety minutes. Even bit players are mentioned, like "the man at the lunch counter."

You can roll the credits and acknowledge the end of your day by reviewing the day's action. Try to recall different people who played a part in your day. Name the cast. Identify the ones who played a starring role because they took up so much of your time. Which bit players achieved a star billing because of your feelings about them?

Get a mental image of the people in your day. Give credit

where credit is due. Then use this next technique to make a connection with your feelings about these characters.

TECHNIQUE: Connect the Feelings

If you can identify and connect with your feelings on the way home from work, you can prevent a disastrous evening. Why waste four hours slamming cupboards or hiding behind a magazine when you could have identified your strongest feelings on your way home?

Here is how this technique worked for a teacher who came home after she found out that her department budget had been cut in half. Her head was pounding, and she was overwhelmed by feelings of anger and disappointment.

But when her husband whistled through the door, she caught herself and said, "Listen, I had a horrible day, and I am inconsolable right now. Anything you say will make me angry or make me cry. I think I'll just stay in bed this evening."

The ending? Her husband, thus alerted, brought her a cool green salad and poached salmon—dinner in bed. Fairy tale? Try this technique and transform your evenings at home.

Practice the technique of identifying and connecting your feelings with the people and events in your day. You can probably identify the people who stirred you; you may find it more difficult to identify the feelings you experienced in those encounters.

When you rolled the credits, you asked yourself about the people who achieved a star billing in your day. In this case, ask yourself: When I left work today, what were my strongest feelings about those people and events?

Then consider a number of words that might express your strongest feelings. Frustration, anger and confusion are common negative feelings in the work arena. But maybe you felt relieved, enthusiastic or optimistic.

My friend and teacher Fred Erickson calls this process "learning the language of emotions." If your habit is to ignore and deny feelings, this connection with them may be a new and unsettling experience.

As you begin to practice identifying and connecting with your feelings, you might want to create or consult a list of words that describes different feelings. With apologies to Barry Manilow, I offer the following "feelings" for your purposes.

AFRAID	DISGUSTED	LISTLESS
AMUSED	DISILLUSIONED	MISERABLE
ANGRY	ELATED	OVERLOOKED
ANGRY WITH MYSELF	EMBARRASSED	PANICKY
ANNOYED	EMPTY	PARALYZED
ANXIOUS	ENERGIZED	POWERLESS
APPREHENSIVE	ENTHUSIASTIC	REJECTED
ASHAMED	ENVIOUS	RELAXED
ASSURED	FREE	RELIEVED
BLAH	FRUSTRATED	RESENTFUL
BORED	FULFILLED	SAD
BURNED	FURIOUS	SKEPTICAL
CAUTIOUS	GRATIFIED	SPITEFUL
COMPETITIVE	GRIEVING	STRONG
CONCERNED	GUILTY	SUCCESSFUL
CONFIDENT	HARASSED	SURPRISED
CONFUSED	HOPEFUL	SUSPICIOUS
CONTENTED	HOSTILE	TENSE
CORNERED	HUMILIATED	THREATENED
CRUSHED	HURT	UNAPPRECIATED
DEPLETED	INDIGNANT	UNCERTAIN
DEPRESSED	ISOLATED	UNEASY
DISAPPOINTED	JOYOUS	USED

A list can help you learn to recognize your expression of feelings. In time, you will quickly identify your version of anger and disappointment. You will know when you are feeling skeptical or overlooked.

Your connection with your feelings about the day is the foundation of any evening at home. When you can label the feelings, you can prevent the evening from being dominated by your unspoken reactions to the events of the day.

Now, how about a nice hot bath?

TECHNIQUE: Bathing with Nancy Reagan

Before Ronald Reagan was elected President in 1980, his wife Nancy told CBS reporter Mike Wallace and millions of viewers about her special technique for coming home from work. Her work in this case referred to her successful career as an attentive political wife.

The technique involved hot baths. In this now famous interview, Nancy revealed her success in cleansing herself of the pressures of political life. But the future First Lady was not referring to the soothing effect of the hot water on her stiff neck or aching feet, nor did she cite the stimulating effects on her circulatory system.

For Nancy Reagan, the most important aspect of bathing involved the conversations she'd have during her bath. Alone in the tub, she would deliver her half of a conversation with one of her husband's political enemies.

She would attack, argue and rebut every innuendo and every enemy on the campaign trail. One by one she would attack them, in the tub, in these imaginary conversations. After these dialogues, she felt cool and removed from the close encounters of the day.

This technique can work for you. Once you have identified both the difficult people you have encountered and your feelings about them, you can draw your own version of Nancy's hot bath. The idea is that you create a situation where you can express your strongest feelings. You have the opportunity to state any angry, witty, sarcastic or uncharitable comments that come to your mind.

Bathing like Nancy Reagan may mean writing a quick and caustic memo that you never send. How about an imaginary conversation on the bus or train home? You can mutter with your office door closed or on the jogging trail. Maybe you can scream in the car (windows closed) on the freeway.

Your version of this technique can cleanse your system of the day's encounters. You will be free to make plans for the evening that do not include the people in the tub.

"HERE'S LOOKING AT ME, KID"

All the techniques in this chapter suggest that you focus on yourself as a first step in your transition from work to home. This phase of coming home can be described as the reversal of a classic Bogart line—almost as if you have been saying to yourself, "Here's looking at *me*, kid."

Before you can look outside of your day at work, you need to acknowledge your hopes and fears about your future. Use these techniques to recognize your feelings about the future and to set those feelings aside on your way home.

TECHNIQUE: Sitting in Breadcrumbs

I talked to a contractor who had a definite image of his worst fears about his future. He elaborated, "I picture myself with nothing to do, sitting on a park bench surrounded by birds and breadcrumbs."

Sometimes we come home from work possessed by our fears of failure or impending catastrophe. We come home carrying the heavy burden of unspoken fears about the future.

Ask yourself: "What is the worst that could happen?" Imagine the most catastrophic outcome for your immediate or distant future. Picture the kind of situation that might leave you "sitting in breadcrumbs."

For example, if I am planning to give a humorous speech on Tuesday, I allow myself to picture an audience of two hundred people, with no one laughing. I cringe when I think of all of them with poker faces, not laughing at a single joke. I see people yawning and looking at their watches.

Usually an extreme fantasy like this makes *me* laugh. But sometimes it allows me to zero in on my exact concern. In this case, maybe I should have picked a safer topic for the Kiwanis Club?

When you recognize your worst unspoken fears, you tend to rob them of their power. This happens because you force yourself to see the exaggerations and distortions in your thoughts about the future.

Yet on other occasions your fears may be genuine. Naming these fears can build a strong bridge to another person. Later I will discuss how to share feelings of failure with people who love you. For now, use this solitary technique as a means of recognizing the unspoken anxieties that can sabotage your evenings at home.

TECHNIQUE: Your Name in Lights

We have talked about the stress and work pressures that haunt your evenings at home. The list included unfinished business and encounters with difficult people. Yet for many of you, the celebration of the day's victories and the prospect of your glittering future may be the source of your self-absorption when you come home.

"When things go well for me at work, that's all I can think about," says one stockbroker. "I am on top of the world and I don't need anybody else!"

If you recognize this feeling, here is an alternative to spending your evenings consumed with fantasies of your brilliant career: Let your imagination soar and imagine the most spectacular outcomes of your present career path. Let yourself recognize your unspoken hopes and dreams; no dream is too vain or unrealistic to be considered.

See yourself selling all of the paintings in your next show, heading the environmental commission or signing that huge contract. Discover a cure for the common cold. Travel to Sweden to collect the Nobel Prize. Remind yourself to write that acceptance speech for Oscar night.

See your name in lights. Let the marquee on Broadway light up with your name and feel your eyes widen with the brilliance of the lights. Smile your most photogenic smile. Then turn off the lights and go home.

Chapter 2
Laughing All the Way Home

"BUT I'M NOT FUNNY"

Did you ever have a friend who comforted you by saying, "Someday, you'll laugh at this"? Were you tempted to answer: "Could you give me an *exact* date?"

"Someday" isn't soon enough; most of us are seeking immediate relief from frustrating or stressful experiences at work. We don't see humor in our situations, and the idea of time adding laughter seems remote.

Each encounter in your day carries the potential for laughter. Yet you find yourself thinking, "But I'm not funny. My parents didn't read to me from Art Buchwald; they read to me from *Bambi*."

Most of us suffer from what the French call "the wit of the staircase," meaning we usually think of something funny after the party or at midnight after work. We think of our witty repartee as we are heading up the staircase—to go to sleep.

You can learn to use humor to change your perspectives about work long before you get home and head up the stairs to go to sleep.

Humor provides the first crucial step in looking outside of experiences at work. As you begin to see your day in a humorous light, you clear the path for others to get close to you. Victor Borge called humor "The closest distance between two people."

This chapter introduces techniques you can use to review the events of your day with a humorous eye. In each, you will review by adding a comic touch to a stressful event that relabels it "funny."

My suggestions are not designed to help you to *be* funny. You won't be ready for open-mike at The Comedy Store, but you will begin to *see* your work in a humorous way. You'll find yourself laughing at mistakes and pressures and creating the prospect of a happier evening at home.

Remember, no one needs to laugh at your inner thoughts and conversations except you. Select and practice the techniques that allow you to reconsider your day in light of your own special sense of humor.

"I LAUGH, THEREFORE . . ."

Let's begin by demonstrating the existence of your sense of humor. Answer these questions carefully.

- Were you the funniest kid in the seventh grade?
- Did parents refuse to let their kids play with you because you knew too many dirty jokes?
- Did you ever get sent to the principal's office because of an attack of giggles?
- Which one of these cartoons makes you laugh: (a) *Peanuts*; (b) *Garfield*; (c) W. Hamilton's *New Yorker* cartoons; (d) Jules Feiffer cartoons; (e) *Doonesbury*.
- Do you have a laugh that is so distinct other people can imitate it?
- Do you ever laugh during R-rated love-making scenes in movies?

- Which one of these shows makes or made you laugh: (a) *The Tonight Show*; (b) *Candid Camera*; (c) *Firing Line*; (d) *Late Night with David Letterman*; (e) *Rowan & Martin's Laugh-In*.
- Do you have a problem remembering a joke's punch line?
- Do you have a problem *understanding* a joke's punch line?
- Which one of these people make you laugh: (a) Joan Rivers; (b) Rodney Dangerfield; (c) Harry Reasoner; (d) Don Rickles; (e) Lily Tomlin.

Analysis: Just being able to answer these questions shows you have a sense of humor. Now consider some unusual techniques that will keep you laughing all the way home from work.

First, try breaking the silence with some special soundtracks.

SOUNDTRACKS

The easiest way to lighten your thoughts about work is to add an imaginary soundtrack to accompany your recollections of the day. You won't need technical skill or a large musical repertoire. Instead, you'll be drawing on your experiences at work and your willingness to hear them with a humorous twist.

As you review your workday you could think of it as a movie or a television show that needs a musical score.

TECHNIQUE: Humming with Rose Mary Woods

All movies and television series use musical scores that set the tone for the show or emphasize a particular mood. For example, the first four notes of the theme from *Dragnet*—dum da dum dum—established the mood of another grim and messy case for Sergeant Friday.

Remember the goofy opening notes of the theme from *Leave It to Beaver* or the jazzy syncopation of *Peter Gunn*? Each of these scores influenced your mood as a viewer of the show.

Comic relief can be achieved by juxtaposing familiar music and lyrics with a stressful or unhappy event. For example, in the film *The Big Chill*, a funeral procession is accompanied by the dead man's favorite song—"You Can't Always Get What You Want" sung by Mick Jagger.

You can borrow this technique. As you rethink frantic, stressful or humiliating moments, add some theme music to provide comic relief.

Consider Rose Mary Woods's situation. Accuracy and confidentiality were her code of honor in her position as secretary to the president. Part of her job was to transcribe taped conversations that took place in her boss's inner office.

Rose Mary was invited to a Senate committee hearing and asked to bring her tapes and notes. Her subsequent testimony revealed her discovery of an astonishing eighteen-minute gap on the tape of a crucial meeting.

We have all misplaced important files and we recognize the feeling that papers or tapes have been snatched by "sinister forces." These feelings suggest the one and only choice as a soundtrack for Rose Mary Woods's day in court.

Her feelings should have reminded her of some of the best episodes of *The Twilight Zone.* As she recalled her day, she could have hummed a few notes of that show's famous theme.

Consider the possibility of adding a musical score as you recall an encounter from your day. Think back to a patronizing conversation you had with your supervisor. Recall how he (or she) explained every detail in pompous, paternal tones.

Now, instead of feeling humiliated when you recall the incident, hum a few bars from Richard Strauss. Specifically, the theme music from the movie *2001*. As you conjure up this soaring, overwrought music, recall your supervisor's patronizing tone. The addition of the music will help you to laugh about what a silly and self-important little man he is.

Imagine the appropriate musical selection as you rethink your day. If you are tone deaf, you can keep some useful theme music to punch into your tape deck.

Each pairing of a stressful incident and a musical interpretation should help transform your feelings about the day. You can practice the technique by matching the events below with an appropriate musical score.

EVENT	SCORE
1. Someone goes over your head to overrule a decision you made.	a. Theme from the movie *Star Wars*.
2. Your co-worker claims credit for your accomplishments.	b. Neil Sedaka singing "Breaking Up Is Hard to Do."
3. You are asked to work overtime for the third time this week.	c. Frank Sinatra singing "I Did It My Way."
4. You are asked to make coffee.	d. Andy Williams singing "Santa Claus Is Coming to Town."
5. Sales arc down and you may be laid off after Christmas.	e. Chopin's "Funeral March" (piano sonata, Opus 35).
6. Your supervisor blames you for her mistakes.	f. Aretha Franklin singing "Respect."
7. One of your partners is trying to erode your power in the firm.	g. Bob Dylan singing "I Shall Be Released."
8. Someone is spreading the rumor that you are sleeping with your assistant.	h. Marvin Gaye singing "I Heard It Through the Grapevine."
9. One of your associates is going through a divorce and you are getting tired of covering for him.	i. The Bee Gees singing "Stayin' Alive."
10. You just missed the deadline for submission of your project report.	j. Title track from the movie *Fame*.

Answers: Any choice is correct if it makes you laugh. Here are some possibilities: (1) c, f; (2) a, j; (3) g, i; (4) f; (5) d, e; (6) g, i; (7) a, j; (8) h; (9) b; (10) e.

Next, listen to the sounds of laughter.

TECHNIQUE: Laugh-tracks

In the 1950s, television introduced us to the experience of "canned laughter." These laugh-tracks were created by recording live studio audiences and were later used by engineers to "sweeten" the soundtrack of a show that had been taped on a closed set.

If you listen to reruns of *Leave It to Beaver* you will hear the same laugh-tracks used over and over again—the roar of an entire audience, scattered chuckling and one lady giggling.

Have you ever wondered how the engineer decided when to plug in the laugh-tracks? Have you heard canned laughter and thought, "I don't get it, what is so funny?"

Laugh-tracks operate on the principle that laughter is contagious. You may not think that something is funny, but if you hear someone else laughing, the sound of the laughter will make you laugh too.

This principle of contagion can work for you on your way home from work. You can rethink your day and decide when you want to "sweeten" your recollections by adding a moment of imaginary canned laughter.

Think back to the tense moments of the day:

- You received your project report back with five pages of suggested revisions.
- At the staff meeting, every solution you presented was greeted with the comment, "It just won't work."
- Your client has just informed you of her intention of hiring another firm to handle her business.

As you review each of these stressful moments, imagine a laugh-track accompanying it. If your imagination fails, you can purchase a cassette with laughter and applause to play in your car or at home.

As you recall your client delivering the fatal blow, imagine peals of laughter. Read through the project report revisions with chuckles in the background, and let giggles overwhelm your memory of negative staff discussions.

Hopefully, the imaginary, incongruous laughter will be irresistible and will accelerate your task of changing and relabeling your feelings about your day.

If not, you can enjoy some purposeful doodling.

CARTOONING

Which one of these cartoons makes you laugh: (a) Peanuts; (b) Garfield; (c) W. *Hamilton's* New Yorker *cartoons;* (d) *Jules Feiffer cartoons;* (e) Doonesbury.

Your choice of cartoon will provide you with strong clues about your sense of humor. You may want to keep a stash of your favorite cartoons to provide comic relief at the end of an exhausting day.

Or you can decide to create some cartoons of your own. As you sit doodling during that last meeting or phone call, try your hand at some comical interpretations of your day.

TECHNIQUE: Two Letter Cartoons

You don't have to be an artist to create comic sketches of your day. In fact, Seattle consultant and artist Michael Buschmohle has evolved a method of cartooning that can be accomplished using the letters H and W.

To use the letter H:

1. Draw the letter H.
2. Add a circle on top.
3. Add arms and feet.

To use the letter W:

1. Draw the letter W.
2. Draw a line across the top.
3. Add a circle on the line.
4. Add arms.

Once you have drawn a simple figure, you can draw simple expressions to convey basic emotions. "Cartoon faces need only eyes and mouths," says Buschmohle. If you decide to include details, you can add a V in the middle of the forehead to emphasize anger or include the person's big nose, Dumbo ears or crow's feet.

You can also add some words to your cartoons.

TECHNIQUE: Balloons

Your cartoons will become more customized and funnier if you include a written message. After you have drawn yourself and another character from work, simply add a balloon coming out of your mouths.

After you have drawn your overbearing co-worker, add a balloon with the words: "The trouble with you is. . . ." Then add a balloon to a picture of yourself and fill it with punctuation marks to denote your X-rated reply: "!!**##!."

Your cartoons and balloon messages provide another opportunity to reexamine your day in a humorous light. Enjoy the laughter and the distance from work you feel. Then quickly shred your drawings and deposit them in the first container you see on the street.

As you continue to look for laughs, you can consult old issues of *TV Guide*.

TV GUIDES

Which one of these shows makes you laugh: (a) Candid Camera; (b) The Tonight Show; (c) Firing Line; (d) Late Night with David Letterman; (e) Rowan & Martin's Laugh-In.

During the last twenty-five years, television has strongly shaped our sense of humor. Your own selection of funny TV shows can provide you with inspiration in the process of reviewing your day. Pick a favorite program and begin to consider your workday as a potential comedy routine on that show.

First, imagine how your day would have looked through the eyes of Allen Funt's hidden camera.

TECHNIQUE: Focus on *Candid Camera*

Remember Allen Funt, the ruddy-faced man who introduced his filmed vignettes as "people being themselves"?

The basic format of *Candid Camera* focused on people in everyday situations *with a twist*. The situation would be manipulated by Funt and his crew to stretch the limits of the person's incredulity.

Classic examples of *Candid Camera* setups included the talking mailbox, the naked lady in the elevator, and the gas station attendant asked to repair a car with no engine.

After the absurd situation had been rolling for several minutes, Funt or one of his staff would appear from behind a door and exclaim: "Smile, you're on *Candid Camera!*"

We never knew which aspect of the filming provoked the strongest reactions in filmed subjects: Was it the sudden reversibility of a crazy situation, the surprise of being filmed for TV or the unexpected idea of sharing an absurd moment with millions of people?

In almost every case, the revelation of the camera's true purpose evoked a mixture of giddy relief. There seemed to be something reassuring in the surprise: "This isn't real, this is television!" Even more important, subjects expressed the thought, "I'm not alone; someone actually *witnessed* this craziness."

The possibility of a hidden camera seems to have become a part of our national consciousness. Listen to Todd describe his ordeal of being relocated within a large bank: "I was going to interview after interview and being asked the same stupid questions. At one interview, I was waiting for Allen Funt to jump out from behind the door!"

As you review your day at work, consider how you might feel if your stressful situations had been setups and were now on film for an episode of *Candid Camera*. Imagine that millions of people had witnessed your colleague's temper tantrum. Share your ordeal with the payroll department's computer in front of countless viewers.

Enjoy the rush of relief you would feel when the camera jumped out of the woodwork. Savor the companionship and the sympathetic chuckles you would evoke from a studio audience.

If you can imagine the hidden camera on your way home from work, you'll have enough material to get *Candid Camera* back on the air.

But maybe you'd rather gather comic material with a famous late-night host.

TECHNIQUE: "Here's Johnny!"

Johnny Carson often enjoys a lively dialogue with his studio audience during his opening monologues. One of the trademarks of this dialogue is that whenever Carson makes a strong statement, the audience eggs him on to exaggerate:

JOHNNY: My dressing room is really small.
AUDIENCE: How small *is* it?
JOHNNY: It is so small I have to step outside to change my mind.

Carson's audience encourages him to exaggerate his descriptions of people and situations and bring humor to the surface. The audience interrupts his complaints and invites him to blow them up to comic proportions.

You can adapt Johnny's techniques to restructure your inner conversations about work. You don't have to *deliver* any of the lines or wait for an audience to laugh. You are the only person who needs to be amused.

Use these four steps:

1. *Identify a difficult person or stressful situation.*
"My boss"

2. *Add an unflattering adjective.*
   "My boss is heartless."
3. *Imagine an audience that asks you:*
   "How heartless *is* he?"
4. *Add an exaggerated comparison.*
   "My boss is so heartless that Idi Amin hired him as a consultant."

Once you have practiced using the structure of this kind of humor, you can easily picture other dialogues with an imaginary audience.

For example:

You:	My presentation was really bad.
Imaginary Audience:	How bad was it?
You:	It was so quiet after I finished that I thought E. F. Hutton had spoken.

Your lines can be as obvious and corny as you please; Johnny's format simply provides a means of organizing and lightening your thoughts about the work.

If you are willing to stay up even later, you can tune in for David Letterman's special brand of humor.

TECHNIQUE: *Late Night with David Letterman*

David Letterman is the serene late-night host of the prosaic. He sees potential for laughter in the most mundane situations, prompting Gloria Steinem to label his show "found humor."

What does he find? "Stupid pet tricks," like the dog who adds, subtracts and multiplies, and people with odd occupations, like Mr. Vincent, who sells maps to the stars' homes from his headquarters near Eva Gabor's tennis court.

He also enjoys placing crank calls on behalf of audience members. "Are you mad at your brother?" Letterman might ask. "OK then, let's call him."

Letterman's mirth is grounded in the celebration of everyday events rather than media events. He's more interested in cele-

brating the anniversary of a couple from Cincinnati than in plug-
ging the opening of a major motion picture.

On your way home from work, you can try to imagine a bit of
"found humor" that Letterman might feature. How about making plans to appear on the show with a time capsule filled with
articles selected from your office?

Your time capsule would be an act of deliberate archeology.
In this case, you would select articles that are representative of
the culture and values of your office. If a future survivor were to
unearth your capsule, he or she would be able to reconstruct life
at work in the 1980s.

Begin your selection of appropriate items. Will you include
your employee handbook, pictures from the office Christmas
party, the transcript from your last trial or some damning inter-
office memos? Do you think you should include your copy of
Dress for Success?

As your selection continues, you will begin to feel a sense of
bemused detachment from the irritating people and unreason-
able expectations of your workplace.

Now, imagine yourself burying the time capsule in Central
Park, on national television, with David Letterman smirking by
your side.

This imaginary appearance on Letterman's show can help you
to find your sense of humor on the way home from work. But if
neither Funt, Carson nor Letterman makes you laugh, consider
some famous one-liners.

TECHNIQUE: Laugh-In

Rowan & Martin's Laugh-In was the top comedy show of the
late 1960s. The show moved at a breakneck pace and was built
on dozens and dozens of one-liners delivered by regulars Goldie
Hawn, Arte Johnson and Lily Tomlin.

The one-line jokes would come at parties, during disco numbers or through portholes at the end of the show. The closing
one-liners were often followed by a suggestion for Dick Martin:
"Say good-night, Dick." As you arrive at the end of your show,
you may want to treat yourself to a series of comic lines that will
help you to say good-night with a smile.

When you sit back and review your day, take a couple of

minutes and search for a one-line joke or insult that accurately describes your sentiments about the people and events in your day. You won't need to hire the staff of *Laugh-In* to add this comic flourish, but you will need to know where the laughs are.

You can build a collection of humor for easy reference at the end of the day.

Some sources you can keep nearby: *Isaac Asimov's Treasury of Humor*, Elaine Partnow's *The Quotable Woman*, Joe Fox's *Trapped in the Organization*, Robert Byrne's *The 637 Best Things Anybody Ever Said*, Nancy McPhee's *The Book of Insults*, John Colombo's *Popcorn in Paradise: The Wit and Wisdom of Hollywood*, Mordecai Richler's *The Best of Modern Humor*, and Herbert Prochnow and Herbert Prochnow, Jr.'s *The Toastmaster's Treasure Chest*.

For a constant source of new materials, subscribe to Joel Goodman's journal *Laughing Matters* and request his bibliography of materials available from The Humor Project in Saratoga Springs, New York.

If this kind of research bores you, maybe you would prefer a comic muse to feed you lines.

PLAY IT AGAIN, RODNEY

Which one of these people makes you laugh: (a) Joan Rivers; *(b)* Rodney Dangerfield; *(c)* Harry Reasoner; *(d)* Don Rickles; *(e)* Lily Tomlin.

In the movie *Play It Again, Sam,* Woody Allen created a marvelous device for his hero—played by Woody Allen. The leading character, Alan, idolizes Humphrey Bogart and can conjure up his presence to serve as a romantic/sexual consultant.

He wants Bogart to feed him specific lines during his awkward and embarrassing moments with women. This is the perfect device for Alan, a man who was "married and still couldn't get a date on New Year's Eve."

In one scene, Alan is trying to kiss Linda (Diane Keaton). Bogart tosses him a line: "Tell her that you have met a lot of dames but she is *really something special.*" Alan says to Bogart,

"That's ridiculous, she'll never believe that." He tells her anyway; she gurgles happily and Alan exalts to Bogart, "She bought it!"

You can invoke a similar kind of adviser to feed you clever lines at the end of the workday. In this case, you probably don't need Humphrey Bogart; you need Rodney Dangerfield.

Choose an appropriate comic adviser and imagine reviewing your day with one of these comics right by your side. Picture your day being attacked with comic bravado by each of these funny people.

JOAN RIVERS

Imagine yourself sitting at your desk at 5:15. A diminutive blonde woman flounces up to you in a black Mary McFadden gown. She pulls up a stool and helps you to look at your day.

Joan Rivers is an ideal after-work adviser because so much of her humor is directed toward the famous and powerful. She feels as comfortable mocking Prime Minister Thatcher ("With humor like hers, you can see how they lost India") as she does roasting Liz Taylor ("She looks at a microwave oven and says, 'Hurry!'").

Joan can help you view the powerful figures in your day with the same streak of comic meanness she reserves for Heidi Abramowitz ("That tramp, she buys pregnancy tests by the six-pack!").

If you refuse to look askance at the people you work with, she will admonish you, "Grow up!!" When you laugh with her, she will stretch her arms out directly in front of her and applaud you.

RODNEY DANGERFIELD

Picture yourself at 5:30, looking for your car in the parking lot. A tall, slouching man with a baggy suit, orange tie and bulging eyes starts muttering beside you:

"I can't get no respect, I called triple A. They wanted to leave the car and tow *me* away."

"Eastern thanked me for flying United."

"No respect, on Halloween I have to trick or treat by telephone."

Rodney Dangerfield is an outstanding adviser when you want to modify feelings of frustration and defeat at work. Conjure up Rodney, tell him what happened and let him know that *you* can't get "no respect," either.

When you borrow Rodney's signature complaint, you immediately give a comic twist to your recollections of the day.

Don Rickles

At 5:15 you hear the sound of someone shouting. You hear toreador music and you see the comedian who respects *no one*. Imagine Don Rickles running up and down the halls of your office building, insulting each person he encounters.

If you choose Don Rickles as an adviser, he will screw up his face like a bulldog and feed you lines in rapid succession. How about joining Don for some old-fashioned, hostile insults at the end of the day?

Send a message to your supervisor via Don: "Fred, with surgery, you could be a great-looking guy. Right now, you look like Roy Rogers without a restaurant."

Lily Tomlin

You pick up the phone at 5:30 and on the other end you hear the voice of Lily Tomlin's most famous character, Ernestine the telephone operator. She asks, "Have I reached the party to whom I *am* speaking?"

Tomlin created Ernestine as a hopeless eavesdropper and an unsympathetic co-worker. She seemed to symbolize the indifference of corporate life.

Imagine telling Ernestine about the horrors of your day. Her comeback: snorting laughter and then, "Well, dear, they are AT&T. They don't care and they don't *have* to!"

Lily Tomlin would be a resourceful adviser at the end of the

day because she can take the guise of many different characters.
For example, she could let her childish character, Edith Anne,
see your office through the eyes of a child. She could have her
character, "the tasteful woman," adjust her hairnet, turn up her
nose and simper: "That's tasteless."

Lily's very human characters can help you to laugh at the
foibles and the pettiness of the characters in your day.

AND AGAIN

You don't need to imagine the *exact* lines these comics would
use. The idea is to borrow each comic's sensibility and look for
moments in your day that he or she would appreciate.

You know that Joan Rivers would scan for office dirt, Dangerfield would look for underdogs, Rickles would tackle the obnox-
ious supervisors and Tomlin would look for office characters she
could imitate.

You can enjoy the companionship of these comic advisers as a
means of helping you to see your day at work in a more humorous, less stressful way.

Every technique and comical intention in this chapter was
designed to help you gain a humorous perspective about the
stresses in your day. If you still aren't convinced about the
power of humor in easing your transition from work, how about
considering the proposition that laughter is a terrific form of
aerobic exercise?

AEROBIC LAUGHTER

During this exercise, your pulse rate doubles, your abdominal
muscles contract, pressure builds in your lungs, your arteries
expand and contract and your endocrine system secretes hor-
mones associated with wiry alertness.

This is not a description of jogging or handball; it is an account
of the physiologic chain of events that begins every time you
laugh.

Laughter adds a new dimension to the idea of a workout. Did you know that air blasting from a laughing person's mouth has been recorded at speeds of up to seventy miles per hour?

According to Mr. William Fry, professor of psychiatry at Stanford University, "Laughing exercises muscle groups all over the body. It is an opportunity for all of us to exercise many times throughout the day. Many people laugh as often as one hundred times each day. There is a difference in degree and intensity— but the exercise adds up over time."

Laughter is one of Dr. Fry's favorite aerobic exercises. "Some people can't jog, but almost everyone, with the exception of those with severe asthma or emphysema, can laugh."

If you are willing to participate in more conventional exercises, the next chapter explores some very good reasons for exercising on your way home from work.

Chapter 3
The Running Slippers

They are no longer fashion news; you have seen them on the streets for several years: elegantly dressed women in dark suits, silk blouses and understated gold jewelry. They are striding toward their cars in waffle-bottomed running shoes.

The origin of this mix-and-match apparel has been the subject of various speculations, including women walking home during the 1981 New York subway strike and the advice given in the book *Thin Thighs in 30 Days*.

These women and their male counterparts (gym bag in one hand, briefcase in the other) are symbolic of the physical transition we make at the end of the day. Perhaps running shoes, rather than ruby slippers, would be the more fitting transitional shoe.

One hundred million Americans, almost half of the population, exercise in some way. And sometimes it seems like the *other* half of the population is making excuses for why they are not exercising.

This chapter introduces four good reasons for making exercise a part of your transition after work and explores three common but unconvincing excuses to avoid working out.

Let's begin with your best intentions.

FOUR PERFECTLY GOOD REASONS TO EXERCISE AFTER WORK

1. Exercise Dissolves Tensions Accumulated During the Day

Walter, a social-services director, describes a tense encounter from his day.

My co-director has no control over his temper. Yesterday, at 4:30, he came into my office and accused me of making a decision without consulting him. He demanded to see copies of all of the letters I had sent out that week.

His attack was so inappropriate and so aggressive, I had to concentrate all of my energy to keep from responding to him.

As Walter listened to his angry colleague, his sympathetic nervous system became aroused and ready to "do battle." At that moment, he was experiencing a series of physical changes that include:

- increased muscle tension
- increased heart rate
- rapid breathing
- marked increase in the secretion of adrenalin
- increased presence of oxygen, fat and cholesterol in the blood.

These physiologic changes are a response to stress that dates back a million years. When our ancient ancestors were faced with a physically threatening situation, they could either fight for survival or run for shelter. This "fight or flight" response has persisted through millions of years of human experience and billions of stressful episodes at work and at home.

An associate's temper tantrum, an impending deadline, a misunderstanding with a client—all of these situations can evoke anger, fear or frustration. But the body doesn't distinguish between physical and emotional threats; whenever you are aroused or stressed, your body reacts with a primeval readiness to do battle.

Dr. James Skinner, professor of physical education at the University of Arizona and author of *Body Energy*, calls this predicament "emotion without motion." He explains: "You are tense and your body prepares you for action; but your job situation doesn't allow you to *do* anything! The tension stays with you and accumulates in your muscles."

"When you exercise," he concludes, "you burn off the accumulated tensions and your body returns to a relaxed state." This is the relaxed state that so many after-work exercisers report.

Walter confirms the experience and has incorporated running after work into his daily routine. "Running is my cocktail. It's my punching bag. It is the way I release all of my tensions from the day. When I run, I expend a lot of energy. I don't seem to be able to run hard and maintain my anger."

Carol, a management consultant, feels the same way about her daily swim. "No matter how tense or angry I am when I get into the pool, I can't seem to hang on to those feelings—even if I try."

And Ted, an attorney for the public defender's office, describes feeling like a "little puppy" after a vigorous Nautilus workout or a competitive squash game. "I have a vigorous workout; I get into the whirlpool and I have gotten it out of my system."

Millions of runners, swimmers, tennis and racketball players and aerobic dancers experience this kind of release from tension through their exercise.

Dr. James Paupst has written in *The Canadian Family Physician* about the symbolic aspect of resolving the fight or flight response through exercise. "All forms of exercise bring on the catharsis, even though it may be symbolic, of the stress reaction. The response *fight* may take place on the squash court; the *flight* may be simulated by jogging through your neighborhood."

2. Exercise Offers Time to Gain Perspective About Work

Repetitive exercises like running, walking, swimming and cycling allow you time to think about the events of your day at work. The exercise period can become a time to connect with your feelings about work and to gain perspective about the day.

Many exercisers report that as they begin to release accumulated tensions, exercise becomes a thoughtful, objective transition time.

Public Defender Ted calls exercise "my only mechanism to detach. During the day, I build up a myopic viewpoint. After exercising, I can see where I was overreacting."

Walter, who deals daily with an angry associate, likes to run with a friend and discuss the day. "As I continue running, I feel myself becoming less emotional, more rational. . . . It feels like a free-flowing catharsis."

And two writers who swim report that ideas for works-in-progress seem to "bubble up" as they move through the water.

3. Exercise Creates a Diversion from Thoughts About Work

For those exercisers who want to *stop* thinking about work, exercise is a definite change of subject. It immediately alters the situational frame.

If you participate in competitive sports like tennis, basketball, handball or squash, you have to concentrate on your opponents, your strategy for the game or signals from team members. The demands of these sports immediately divert your attention from work problems.

"If I start thinking about the pile of papers on my desk—and I don't watch the ball—I'll lose," said one tennis player.

This shift in focus gives you time out from reliving and obsessing about your experiences at work. The exercise environment itself can provide a diversion.

The colored leotards in your aerobic dance class, the sound of a basketball hitting the wooden court, the smell of chlorine in the swimming pool, each of these environments provides a sharp contrast to the sensory experiences of your workday.

If you exercise outdoors, your attention may shift to other stimuli. Donna, a physician, explains, "Being outside feels different and I experience myself in a different way: I listen to birds, I say hello to people, I pet dogs."

4. Exercise Provides an Opportunity for Private Time

Although many exercisers enjoy the companionship of a basketball game or a running partner, others cherish exercise as precious time alone before facing a spouse or family at home.

"I figured out that I come in contact with over one hundred people a day," says a cardiologist. "I used to enjoy playing squash, but now I find that I need to run by myself. I really need that time *alone*."

Dan Oliver, director of physical fitness for the Weyerhaeuser Company, tells a story about a manager who was approached by someone who worked for him while he was exercising in the company's physical fitness center. He told the employee, "This is *my* time. If you've got a question about business, I'll meet you in thirty minutes at my desk."

Karen, an advertising copywriter, elaborates on this theme. "I do tasks and projects for other people all day. When I come to the gym, I change my clothes and take off my glasses; I get a fuzzy outlook as I go through my exercise routine. No one knows me here, I can be as self-centered as I please."

In spite of all of the good reasons, you may not be exercising after work. You'll recognize the popular excuses that follow, and maybe you'll be willing to practice some techniques to refute them.

THREE COMMON BUT CONVINCING EXCUSES

1. "I Am Too Tired"

Cora, a schoolteacher and small business owner, is familiar with this excuse. "I get to school at about 7:30 A.M. and by the time I get home, my choice is to exercise or to go to bed. It is always a big mistake to stop by the house to change. I see the bed, the darkened bedroom—the last thing in the world I want to do is to go to my exercise class!"

Like Cora, at the end of the day you may feel "too tired" to exercise. You assume that this means that you don't have the energy to exercise and that if you do, you'll need to be carried out of the gym on a stretcher.

But remember that many of the sensations that you label as "being tired" are part of the tension accumulated from your inability to act on the fight or flight phenomenon. Your body is housing a day's worth of unexpressed tensions.

In addition, you may have been sitting still during much of

the day and your body's systems are operating at a sluggish rate. When you exercise, you will relieve accumulated tension and stimulate sluggish systems.

Dr. James Skinner explains that every form of exercise places demands on various parts of the body and the body responds to these demands, producing the sensation of stimulation and the energy you feel after exercise.

Aerobic exercises, like swimming, jogging, cycling, jumping rope and handball, have been found to produce the greatest stimulation of your cardiovascular system.

All of the evidence points to the fact that moderate exercise will make you feel more alert, *less* tired. The trick is to remember how energized you felt when you exercised yesterday.

TECHNIQUE: Yesterday's Workout

"Ask me if I am looking forward to working out," said the woman standing at the locker next to mine. "I'm not; but I sure am looking forward to the way I'll feel *afterward.*"

The expectation of the benefits of exercise can help bridge the gap between fatigue and participation. The more you exercise, the more you can draw upon positive memories to motivate yourself.

"I am always glad I came to class, *after* class," said one aerobic dancer.

The technique, then, is to recall how you felt *after* the last time you exercised. Try to get a mental image of yourself after your run or swim or tennis game. Picture yourself after your shower, feeling relaxed and energized. See yourself bounding down the street, on your way home.

Remember, if you exercise after work, you will avoid bringing guilt home with you. Marie-Anne, a college administrator, confessed: "If I don't exercise, I just come home and plop down in front of the TV. If I do exercise, I might plop down anyway. But at least I don't feel *guilty.*"

2. *"I Can't Afford One of Those Expensive Health Clubs"*

This excuse is reasonable enough. Those who belong to health clubs feel that the initial financial bite and the dues are worth the benefits of a regular location for exercise and the added bonuses of sauna, whirlpool or steam room.

Money may be a reason you can't take a sauna after work, but it is an unconvincing reason for skipping exercise altogether. Yoga, walking, running and calisthenics don't require a large investment. And for under $100 you can buy an aerobic exercise record, a rebounder trampoline, a bicycle, a jump rope, a set of weights or a stationary bike.

Nancy, a public-health nurse, invested in a rowing machine. She has a circle of friends who buy and trade home exercise equipment. This month she is looking forward to borrowing a small trampoline.

And don't be a snob. The YMCA, YWCA or local community center probably has a pool, weight room, handball courts and aerobic dance classes. Do you really need to be seen in the locker room of a fancy downtown athletic club?

POSSIBILITY: A Company Workout

If you are lucky, your company may have some athletic facilities you can use. George Feiffer, director of the Health Management Program at Xerox and president of the Association for Fitness in Business, reports that there are 440 fitness centers in companies across the country. Companies like PepsiCo, Johnson & Johnson, Bonne Bell, Weyerhaeuser and Chase Manhattan Bank have fitness centers backed by a corporate philosophy emphasizing the importance of exercise.

If your company is large and in reasonably good financial standing, you might consider organizing a group of employees to lobby for a company fitness center.

Arm yourself with convincing statistics, like those listed under "Consumer Alert" in the December 1983 issue of *American Health*.

- Employees in exercise classes at Nebraska Northern Gas Company use one-fifth less sick days than other employees.
- New York Telephone reported statistics resulting from addition of a fitness center: $6.5 million savings in medical bills, $1 million saved in overtime, and 0.9 percent reduction in hospital costs.

Dr. Kenneth Pelletier's book *Healthy People in Unhealthy Places* should provide additional information.

If a company-wide program seems impossible, you could organize a group of employees to chip in and hire an aerobic dance teacher or a yoga instructor and schedule classes within your work setting at the end of the day.

And—if all else fails—you can do exercises while you are sitting at your desk.

TECHNIQUE: At Your Desk

Rena Ettlinger of Rena's Gyms in Chicago has developed a series of exercises that can be practiced while you are sitting at your desk or waiting for an elevator.

The first four exercises can be done in a seated position. They are designed to reduce fatigue caused by tired shoulders and a stiff neck.

1. Sit straight in your chair with feet flat on the floor. Lift arms above your head with elbows locked and palms facing each other. Reach upward until whole rib cage lifts. Now, bend down from the waist, reaching toward your ankles. Relax. Repeat five times.

2. Sitting on the edge of your chair, put your knees together with feet flat on the floor. Put your hands behind you on the seat with your elbows locked. Arch your back and lift your hips off of the chair. Tighten buttocks and let your head drop back. Repeat five times.

3. Sit back in your chair with hands clasped behind your head. Lean forward and touch your right elbow to your left knee. Then touch your left elbow to your right knee. Return to starting position and alternate five times.

4. Sit straight in your chair with your legs together. Raise and straighten one leg directly in front of you. Point your toe and flex your foot backward and forward. Rotate your ankle in the flexed position. Circle to the right, then circle to the left. Alternate legs and repeat five times.

The next two exercises can be done while you are standing next to your desk or waiting for an elevator. The movements reverse the positions you have been sitting in all day.

1. Raise your arms above your head with hands clasped close to your ears. Keeping elbows locked, bend over to the right as far as possible. Bend to the left. Repeat five times on each side.

2. Hold on to your desk or a wall to maintain straight posture. Do not lean. Standing straight, flex your right foot up (heel down, toes pointed toward your head). Raise leg out to the side (it will not go very far). Hold to the count of ten. Repeat with left leg.

Although areobic exercise is generally believed to be the most energizing of all workouts, any kind of exercise that allows for stretching and bending can help relieve the tension and stiffness that result from sitting at a desk all day.

Ms. Ettlinger suggests that these exercises be followed by a "brisk walk to your car."

3. "I Don't Have Time to Exercise After Work"

Time is a precious commodity after work. When you have to put family and domestic responsibilities on hold, it is difficult to justify exercise time. You may see exercise as an indulgence you can't afford. Or you may find that exercising after work will make your evenings too short.

But consider the idea that over a period of time exercise takes less time than the family fights and sour evenings that are a result of coming home from work with unrelieved stress. Exercise can't make up for lost time; but the quality of time that you spend with your family and friends may improve significantly. You may echo Karen's sentiments.

"Driving home from work just isn't enough time to unwind. The day just sits there with me; I pack it in my briefcase. If I exercise, I get home later; but I walk out of the gym focused on what I am going *to* instead of what I have come from."

Even so, exercise can be a logistical impossibility. If this is the case, consider some other alternatives:

- *Walking home.*
  Consult *The Complete Book of Exercise Walking* by Gary Yanker.

- *Parking in a distant lot that allows you a long walk after work.*
  This option will entail slipping out of your Lois Lane pumps or stiff-backed wing tips.

- *Jumping rope on your living room rug for twelve minutes.*
  Invest in a good jump rope like one from AMF Whitely Physical Fitness Products. Jump for 15 seconds, rest for 45 seconds.

- *Exercising with a spouse, friend or lover.*
  Combine exercise time and social time. If you want to exercise at home, consult *Working out Together* by Carol MacGregor.

- *Exercising during lunch.*
  Merie Hannon, exercise physiologist at Chase Manhattan Bank, says that noon is the peak time for using the corporate gym. At noon, you can burn off the accumulated tensions of the morning, and exercise at *any* time of the day will increase your tolerance of stress.

- *Involving your children in an exercise program.*
  Dan Oliver, at the Weyerhaeuser Corporation, reports that spouses and children are encouraged to come to the exercise facility at noon and after work. If your time crunch involves children, have them meet you at the health club or community center. Or plan exercise time together when you get home, using exercise records or cassettes. Let each person exercise at his or her own pace.

- *Involving the family in your sports league.*
  Make your softball game a family outing with dinner before or ice cream afterward.

- *Eating a large lunch to cut down preparation time of elaborate dinners.*
  Instead, spend the usual preparation time exercising and coming home to a snack or light dinner.

NOURISH THE BEAST

Mavis is a record company's talent manager with a long commute home. "I sit on the freeway—half starved—for twenty-five minutes. By the time I get home, I am so hungry and cranky that I can barely say hello."

"When your stomach is empty, its walls are being irritated by acidic juices," explains Dr. Brian Morgan at Columbia University's Institute of Nutrition. "Your stomach is contracting on itself."

A hungry person, like Mavis, will describe herself as feeling uncomfortable, nauseated or irritable. This is obviously not the beginning of an enchanted evening.

Dr. Harvey Katzeff, assistant professor of medicine at New York Hospital–Cornell Medical Center, believes that physical fatigue at the end of the day may be partly attributed to "coming down from a caffeine high created by multiple cups of coffee and scanty eating.

"At this point, the worst possible choice would be a diet cola that contains caffeine with no calories or nutrients. The cola will provide a temporary pickup that will deplete the glycogen in the liver and contribute to later feelings of fatigue and nausea."

Virtually anything a hungry person eats will reduce hunger pangs, and surprisingly few nutritionists are willing to suggest the existence of "high energy" foods.

Most nutrition experts, like the University of Washington's Dr. Bonnie Worthington-Roberts, say that the problem with so-called junk foods is that they *do* satisfy hunger: "They supply calories without nutrients. If you eat a snack with these empty calories, you will lose your appetite for dinner and deprive yourself of needed nutrients."

AN APPLE A DAY

Drs. Morgan, Katzeff and Worthington-Roberts all agree that a apple would be an ideal snack on the way home from work.

The apple received uniformly high marks for nutrients, fibrous matter and quick absorption into the bloodstream. Other fruits, vegetable sticks and cheese and crackers were also strong choices.

The message: Keep an apple on your dashboard or in your desk; stock your refrigerator with fruits and preprepared vegetable sticks for immediate relief from hunger pangs.

HAPPY HOUR: CAN IT REALLY MAKE YOU HAPPY?

An editor confessed to a friend over lunch, "Things are getting really bad at the paper; I had to have two drinks before going home last night."

Happy hour, with its low-priced drinks and salty hors d'oeuvres, is a regular part of many working people's routines. Those who imbibe report increased feelings of relaxation and well-being.

The happiest part of the hour may have little to do with alcohol. You can enjoy the festive mood of a crowd in which each person is trying to relax after work; you may unwind by talking about your day with the bartender or with your companions. Still, you'll want to remember the facts about alcohol.

Research regarding alcohol use has documented the facts that after one or two drinks, alcohol affects the brain as a stimulant. Beyond that limit, alcohol acts as a depressant and you may begin to feel agitated, saddened or frustrated rather than becalmed.

Changes in behavior may depend on how quickly alcohol is absorbed into your bloodstream. If you plan to continue drinking during happy hours, take these factors into account:

- *Order a plate of apples and cheese.*
  An empty stomach will increase the speed with which alcohol is absorbed into the bloodstream.

- *Sip your Irish coffee slowly.*
  Warm alcohol is absorbed more quickly than cold alcohol.

- *Try to mix with water or fruit juice.*
  Mixers like water and fruit juice slow the process of alcohol absorption. Carbonated mixers, like colas and club soda, speed it up.

A handful of the techniques from earlier chapters and thirty minutes on the tennis court may eventually replace a three-drink happy hour in your plans for the evening.

EXERCISE BRINGS YOU CLOSER TO HOME

When you exercise, you experience a physical unwinding, a diversion from your thoughts about work and the opportunity for private time. Exercise can contribute to feelings of relaxation and renewed energy.

The physical stimulation and release of tensions can contribute to feelings of distance from your thoughts about your day. In this way, exercise brings you closer to home.

Chapter 4

"Honey, I'm Home"

STALKING THE GREAT WHITE WHALE

You probably encountered your first case of job burnout in high school. Whether you read the original or the Cliff's Notes edition, you learned about Captain Ahab and his obsessive search for Moby Dick.

Remember his classic symptoms: self-absorption, exhaustion and loss of humor. Living on the boat seemed to aggravate the problem; no opportunity to exercise or to gain distance from work, dating was out of the question and whale jokes—you can be sure—were absolutely taboo.

Those of you who spend your days presenting "killer ideas," "tackling new projects" and "knocking them dead," may recognize Ahab and yourself in the words of this government project engineer. "When I am working on a really hot project, I think nothing of working eighteen hours a day. Eating, sleeping and sex are not important."

In this chapter, you'll have the opportunity to sample techniques that will allow you to shift attention away from yourself and to express a loving interest in your family and friends.

Let's begin with your world view.

AS THE WORLD SHRINKS

Have you noticed that most TV soap operas revolve around the details of people's lives at work? Hospitals and oil conglomerates are favorite settings. Inside these workplaces, millions of enthralled viewers witness the tiniest details of mergers, typing errors and unnecessary surgery.

Focusing on the small world of the workplace is nothing new to most of us. As we travel home from work, we are preoccupied with the small, maddening details that soap opera writers adore: We can report every word of a peppery phone conversation, name each person who voted to reduce the program budget and confirm rumors of office affairs, both the poignant and the expedient.

In addition, you have probably spent your day focusing on a series of specific tasks. With your nose to the grindstone, you may have assigned great importance to budgets, quotas and forecasts.

The world tends to shrink as you focus on these people and events at work. Perspective is lost when you tie your sense of well-being to a small number of people and a small collection of details.

The next three techniques are designed to expand your shrinking world and to increase perspective about your day.

TECHNIQUE: Headlining

Try the most obvious antidote for a shrinking world view: stop at the newsstand or turn on the news.

Pause at the newsstand and reread the headlines of the day. You may be surprised to learn that the story of the power struggle in your office is not front-page news. Linger for a moment and think about how the headlined events affect other people.

Turn on National Public Radio as you drive and contemplate problems of an immense scale: world hunger, natural disasters, nuclear disarmament. Ask yourself, "What are the consequences, on a global scale, of my failure to land the Sears account?"

This approach allows you to hit yourself over the head with the obvious. It is permissible to think in clichés as you read the headlines. You could include, "my problems are really very small" or "life goes on without me." You might ask, "Is my cup half empty or half full?"

Now try the next technique and move from fact to fiction.

TECHNIQUE: Science Fiction

Unexpected encounters with the future are a frequent theme in science fiction. Rod Serling and H. G. Wells have delighted us with characters who were catapulted into the future.

The future is *the* dimension that will change your feelings about today's work. (See also "But I'm Not Funny," page 34.) The passage of five or ten years will soften the impact of your present sense of catastrophe.

But why wait for ten years? You can employ the technique of a science fiction writer to project yourself into the future and to create a healing distance from your day at work.

You don't need to possess the literary gifts of H. G. Wells. Instead, substitute imagination and your knowledge of your workplace to create a fictional future.

Kathleen, a public relations consultant, begins her futuristic tale with a question: "In 1995, how important will it be that my slides jammed in the projector and I had to reschedule my presentation?"

Continue to create your future. Picture your clients or your supervisor ten years from now; see each person ten years older and ten pounds heavier. Who in your office is the most likely candidate for a toupee? Which of your clients will be getting estimates for a face lift?

The goal is to remember that as time passes, perspective changes. You don't need to wait for time to create distance from your feelings; you can envision the future on your way home from work.

If you prefer to reserve your literary efforts for the novel in your desk, try the next technique. You can use space, rather than time, to create distance from your work.

TECHNIQUE: Gaining Altitude

The court date was Wednesday, and Grant had memorized every word of his opening statement. He had rehearsed every possible question and anticipated any objections. He was thinking, "If I don't win this case, I'll have to spend another year as a junior associate!"

Each of you has experienced this pressure to perform. The pressure increases as you get closer to the demands and challenges of your job. Your stress level multiplies as you become strongly identified with the outcome of a particular task.

At times, you may feel as if every decision and every problem on paper is written in capital letters. As you begin to examine your work too closely, you become cross-eyed.

Try the experience of an imaginary plane ride as a technique that allows you to gain distance from your emotional investment in the people and projects at work.

- Book yourself on a fantasized flight that departs from a ramp connected to your desk. Settle into your chair, fasten your seat belt and prepare for your departure.
- Imagine your plane gaining altitude. Look out your imaginary window and see your desk growing smaller below you. Within seconds you will be unable to read any of the papers on it.
- Watch the people becoming smaller and smaller. You can no longer see the expression on your supervisor's face. In fact, he is beginning to look like a tiny plastic marker on a game board.
- From this distance, the people and the projects will look very small and you will be far above the fray. Try to enjoy the view while you can.

With your new gains in perspective, you'll be ready to focus on the important people waiting for you at home.

CUTTING EINSTEIN'S STEAK

I once had a relationship with David, a scientist who tried to excuse his absorption in work by telling me a story that cannot possibly be true. He insisted that when Einstein sat down at the dinner table, he remained so preoccupied with the mysteries of the universe that his wife had to cut his meat for him!

I refused to believe that Einstein's universe could be so small. But apparently the purpose of this story was a metaphor that explained why David spent so many of *our* dinners sketching the design for his next experiment on my cocktail napkin.

The message: If someone is doing important work, then everyone else must put their own needs aside and allow the great one to continue working.

Do you carry home a similar inflated idea of the importance of your work? Would you like to be working/living a kind of seamless existence interrupted only by meals and the sound of someone else cutting your food?

The problem develops because we spend the day at work absorbed in ourselves: our ideas, our decisions, our career opportunities. Work is the essence of self-absorption; in the act of concentration, we attempt to block out the thoughts and feelings of others so that we can focus on our own ideas.

The key to the transition between work and love is developing the capacity to shift from a concentration on yourself to a warm and responsive focus on the important people at home.

The fantasy that we all share is that once we are home, just the presence of family and friends will allow us to leave the day behind. We also believe that if we really love someone, the transition will happen magically.

Jed, a painter, explains his disillusionment: "I always thought that when I got married, I would easily leave my studio and the thoughts about my paintings behind. I thought this would happen spontaneously. Do I really have to make an *effort* to respond to her?"

Don't assume that it is natural or easy to turn away from your thoughts about work and focus on the people who care about you. Instead, plan to make a genuine effort to become emotionally available at the end of the day.

Each of the techniques in this section requires that you make an effort to visualize, concentrate and speculate about people and events outside of your experiences at work and progress toward a focus on your loving family and friends.

Let's start by eavesdropping.

TECHNIQUE: **Eavesdropping**

I was racing to the printer, with five minutes before closing time. Without my materials, tomorrow's workshop would be a fiasco. I rushed into the elevator, groping for Excedrin in my purse and feeling sorry for myself.

An elegant couple stepped into the elevator and began this conversation:

HE: But sometimes you can do "one more for the gip-per?"

SHE: Yeah, I just say: "As long as I don't have to move."

I began to eavesdrop shamelessly as I walked out of the elevator, wondering: Are they married? Friends? Lovers? Is this dialogue from a 1940s movie? Then I laughed, realizing that for one brief, voyeuristic moment I had forgotten my own pressures and complaints.

Eavesdropping deserves a four-star rating as a means of reducing self-absorption. It is a technique that can be used wherever you are in close proximity to other people. Elevators, bus stops, crosswalks, subways and supermarkets are all prime locations.

Allow your ear to wander and listen to someone else complain about their day, make plans for the evening or try to recover from a bad date. The key is getting momentarily absorbed in *another* person's world.

Chances are that you will listen to someone complain about their day in a way that mirrors your own feelings. This can help to remove your fatigue and pressures from the realm of cruel and unusual punishment. And for one moment you will have stepped away from your day.

One caution: During a recent lecture I gave, an audience member reminded me that our parents taught us that it was rude to eavesdrop. Let me amend that lesson and say that it would be rude to *interrupt* when eavesdropping. Imagine if I had said to the couple in the elevator, "Excuse me, but I think faking enjoyment in sex is a real mistake!"

But if you think eavesdropping is rude, I don't know what you'll think of the next technique. It involves staring.

TECHNIQUE: Supermarket Speculation

Isn't it irritating to stand in line at the supermarket at the end of the day? For most of us, the long lines at the market are added to our grocery list of complaints about the day. But rather than fuming in line, why not practice a technique that continues the process of gaining distance from the day?

Let your eyes focus on the carts in front and on either side of you. Take a quick inventory of the items: Pampers and Gerbers. Tab, cottage cheese and tuna. Carnations and kielbasa. Macaroni and freeze-dried potatoes.

Now try three different kinds of speculation.

First, you can try to figure out facts about the person's life at home just from looking at the items in their cart. Is this person single, married or at home with a baby? Is he binging on chocolate or trying the Fiber Diet? Is she planning a wedding, a party or a poker game?

You can go even further. Test yourself by looking at the cart and then guessing who is pushing it. For example, if you see two steaks, salad fixings and a bottle of wine, you can guess a couple on a date. If the cart contains five boxes of plastic baggies, you are probably waiting in line with a marijuana dealer.

See if you agree with the person's menu planning. Boneless chicken breasts (good idea, saves time), fresh mushrooms, real butter and half-and-half (that sauce might be too rich), and brussels sprouts (terrible mistake, didn't he see the fresh asparagus?).

While you concentrate on conversations and groceries, you look outside of your own day. Then you're ready to focus on your family and friends.

TECHNIQUE: Glimpsing

As you prepare to greet your family or friends, you can begin by creating a series of mental images that allow you to put these important people in clear focus.

For example, you can start with short glimpses of your wife's face. Fill in her eyes, eyelashes and eyebrows; outline her smile. Count her freckles and her wispy, occasional gray hairs. Imagine taking your finger and touching the tip of her nose.

Try to hold each of the images as long as you can. If you have difficulty creating a mental picture, carry a family photo in your wallet or take a close look at the framed portrait on your desk.

Now shift your thinking to recall leaving home earlier today.

Were you both feeling angry about an unresolved argument? Did you linger at breakfast with warm, confiding conversation? Did you leave looking forward to a quiet evening or to a discussion of a visit to her parents?

Change your focus and begin thinking about her day. What plans did she have for the day? What frustrations or triumphs might she be bringing home? Picture her at home; what could she be feeling at this exact moment?

Take the time and picture each person you will greet at home. If you are on your way to meet a friend, use the same techniques to ease your approach.

The practice of glimpsing provides your first connection with your loved ones at the end of the day. It can expand your capacity to focus outside of your own experiences and to become an empathic, responsive partner.

Now consider just one more thought before you walk through the front door.

TECHNIQUE: The Thought That Counts

When you see someone carrying flowers at 5:15, you can be sure they have taken at least three minutes away from their own thoughts to focus on a gift for a special person.

If you stop to shop for a gift, you give yourself time out from your myopic thoughts about work. You are forced to ask yourself, "What would he/she like?"

You don't need to splurge. How about his favorite candy bar, a Mylar balloon, a photocopy of an article she would enjoy or a box of strawberries in the middle of winter?

Since you won't arrive bearing gifts every day, try window shopping as an active substitute. As a means of focusing on a friend or lover, ask yourself: "If I could bring Sam a present, what would it be?"

Walk quickly past store windows and choose a shirt that would be just right with his new sport coat. Select a soft leather briefcase to replace his worn-out edition. Cruise a gourmet deli and consider bringing home the pumpkin tortellini.

As you select your real or imaginary gifts, you begin to connect with the affection and delight you want to express when you walk through the front door and greet your family.

GREETINGS: THE FIRST THREE MINUTES

You can ruin an entire evening just by saying hello. Consider this scenario: David is a college professor who found out today that his research grant would not be renewed for next year. He comes home exhausted, after spending the day scrambling to find alternative sources of funding.

6:01   David walks through the door, looking forward to an evening with Jenny, but he is so tired that he gives her a half-hearted hug.

6:02   Jenny moves toward David, anticipating a kiss. As the recipient of an unenthusiastic hug, she feels rebuffed and slightly angry.

6:03   Jenny berates David for not stopping at the cleaners. She starts reading the newspaper, treating David with indifference, and gives up her fantasy of making love later that evening.

6:04   David is confused and angry about Jenny's aloof response. He tells her he needs to work in his study after dinner.

Obviously, both the marriage and the evening can be saved. But David had neglected to do the basic "homework" that has been outlined. If he had reviewed and explored his feelings about work, he would have been capable of *separating* his feelings. David needed to separate his feelings on two fronts: (1) He was happy to see Jenny; (2) he felt frustrated and exhausted from his day at work.

Mike is a surgeon who summarized greeting from the two fronts with wit and accuracy: "After a particularly horrible day,

I'd say to her, two things I want you to know: One is that I love you, and two is that if you come anywhere near me, I will knock your block off!"

Warm greetings, when accompanied by hugs and kisses, can be expressed in twenty-five words or less.

"What a day, it's good to be home."

"I am ready to murder my secretary, but I'm glad to see you."

You can survive the first three minutes at home by making your greetings pleasant and by postponing discussion of the day's horrors. Then you can practice the next two techniques and request some quiet time alone.

TECHNIQUE: "I Want to Be Alone"

The desire for time alone is one reason many people work late in their offices. After others go home, they find time for reflection and for review of the day's events. The demand for time alone when you come home should be a delicate negotiation. In reality, it seldom works that way.

Donna, a purchasing manager, wryly reports: "My husband wants me to put a drink in his hand, give him his paper, put him in his lounger, blow his nose and leave him alone!"

You are entitled to some quiet time when you come home from work. The question is how you communicate your need. You cannot simply announce that, like Garbo, you "want to be alone," and then disappear for a two-hour champagne bubble bath.

Let your husband and children know that you are happy to see them. Then you can convince them that your time alone reflects your own needs and not your feelings about them.

Robin, a local news personality, offers this approach: "When I come through the door, I put on a smock and for ten minutes my husband, the kids and the dog can jump all over me. Then I retire to my room to spend some time alone."

A mutual vow of silence can substitute for time alone.

If you anticipate the need for silence, you can simply ask for it. Silence can prevent your evening from gathering negative momentum.

Celia, an administrative assistant, told me, "Last week I had such a bad day that I kissed Steve and asked if we could maintain radio silence for the first hour."

You can develop a large repertoire of relaxing rituals for your silent or solo time. Each of these activities will ease your entry through the front door.

Try playing music, petting the cats, working on a crossword puzzle, snacking on cheese and crackers, reading the mail, starting a fire in the fireplace, watering the plants, puttering in the garden, reading magazines or newspapers, watching the home team, taking a swim or a shower, retreating to a hot tub or sauna, listening to music, walking the dog, giving or getting a massage, playing electronic games, doing needlepoint or woodcraft, watching reruns of *Mary Tyler Moore*, browsing in store catalogues or shopping by mail.

Practice techniques in this book or do something you read about in a frivolous magazine: put cucumbers, tea bags or shredded potatoes on your face. Then stretch out on your bed and take a ten-minute catnap.

As you ease into the evening, you will be asking an important question.

WHAT'S FOR DINNER?

Unless you enjoy making pasta from scratch at the end of an eight-hour day, you probably are struggling to find a method for getting dinner on the table quickly.

You have read that frozen entrees are a multimillion-dollar business, so you know that somewhere, someone isn't cooking at night. Let's assume that you don't expect to prepare a seven-course meal and that if both of you are working, you will both participate in cooking.

Consider seven different solutions, not including TV dinners, that couples and singles can use to remove mealtime as grounds for divorce or hermitage.

Review your own experiences with each method.

METHOD	ADVANTAGES (+)	DISADVANTAGES (−)
1. Takeout food	Provides instant gratification of ethnic food cravings.	Takes on the flavor of Styrofoam while the container leaks in your lap.
2. Cuisinart or Veg-O-Matic	Allows you to dice, slice and shred your dinner in sixty seconds.	Takes longer to clean than it does to use.
3. Crock-Pot or slow cooker	Works the same eight hours that you do.	If you unexpectedly work late, your chili con carne will be reduced to pabulum.
4. Cooking for the entire week	Virtually eliminates preparation time.	Ruins Sunday afternoons, since you must watch whatever is bubbling on the stove or roasting in the oven.
5. Microwave oven	Produces hot, home-cooked meals with astonishing speed.	You watch nervously for the surgeon general's report confirming the long-range damaging effects of microwaves.

METHOD	ADVANTAGES (+)	DISADVANTAGES (−)
6. Stanislav, the Russian émigré-turned-chef	Can have steaming borscht and a flawless beef Stroganoff waiting for you.	His salary is outrageously high and he increases your ambivalence about detente.
7. Eating in restaurants	White tablecloth, candlelight; you do not have to prepare the dishes or wash them.	Slow service and being forced to learn the first name of your waiter or waitress.

WINE TASTING

In Napa Valley, a certain expression is used to describe a wine with complex taste. Last summer, I was handed my fifteenth sample of Chardonnay with the introduction: "This wine has a long finish."

I hesitated for a moment, picturing farm workers striking for health-care benefits. I tasted the wine and understood the expression immediately. As I sipped, the wine offered three distinct tastes in rapid succession: sweet, tart, mellow.

The techniques in the past four chapters are designed to structure a "long finish" to your workday. If you have read and practiced the techniques, you should be enjoying a heightened awareness and a sense of relief.

Now you are ready to answer the next question: "How was your *day?*"

Part
TWO

SHOP TALK

Chapter 5

"How Was Your Day?"

I *sland*, Aldous Huxley's utopian spoof, chronicles the business trip of Will Faraday, a British journalist who has been sent to the Southeast Asian island of Pala to scout oil leases for his publisher.

On this most unusual business trip, Will encounters a storm in the straits of Pala. His boat is smashed on the beach and he scrambles up the island cliffs. Unnerved by the sight of a snake, he falls, but survives.

The first island resident he meets is a ten-year-old girl who suggests that he use a popular island technique for altering his traumatic memories. With crisp authority, she insists that he tell her the story of the storm, the shipwreck and the snake at least one hundred times. She is not satisfied until the memory loses its powerful effect on Will.

Huxley's island lore bears a resemblance to some of the techniques recommended in earlier chapters. The difference is that the techniques are meant to be practiced *alone*. You would not expect family and friends to listen to your raw, unprocessed feelings about the day, nor would you ask them to listen to the same story over and over.

As an alternative to being stranded on a tropical island, this chapter introduces the art of editing your thoughts and feelings about work *before* sharing them with family and friends. Editing is guided by the "share but spare" principle of communication.

The wisdom of this editorial principle comes from a familiar teenage plea: *"Spare me the gory details!"* Tools for editing "the details" include timing, translation, accuracy, shading and humor.

You may object and say, "But my wife—or friends—and I share everything."

I am not talking about withholding feelings, I am questioning the wisdom of expecting others to sort out your feelings *for* you. It is essential to have done the "homework" in previous chapters. If you have practiced a handful of techniques, you will have labeled your own feelings and gained in perspective about the day.

The feelings you share can be edited in a way that makes them easy to follow and can lead to an intimate exchange with family and friends. Besides, if you can talk about work in an intense and pointed way, you'll have more time for other playful and intriguing topics.

Before you practice editing, take care to select the right person for conversation.

TECHNIQUE: Talking to the Bartender

Talking to the bartender has become a cliché of homecoming cartoons. The bartender is someone who has no investment in what you say; he will not be hurt by your words, nor can he hurt you. He is an impartial observer.

If you don't talk to the bartender, who is the right person? For Denise, a small business owner, the right person is a colleague in the same field but not the same office. David, an insurance agent, confides in the one man he trusts in his division.

You may find comfort in talking to someone who—unlike your family—understands the unique peculiarities of your work situation and may even know some of the same people, but I would caution you to evaluate the risks of confiding your perspectives to someone in your workplace.

We often hear the expression "my friend at work." Just as

frequently, we hear a story about confidences betrayed by former friends on opposite sides of an issue. Donna's story is a case in point.

Donna was a faculty member who enjoyed a close friendship aftr work with Lynn, a member of the same department. Donna had confided her doubts about the priorities of the Sociology Department and her lack of confidence in the department chairman.

That summer, following drastic budget cuts, Lynn lost her position and Donna remained with a part-time teaching role. During the jockeying for position that preceded the budget cuts, Donna learned that Lynn had passed on Donna's confidential viewpoints in hope of making herself appear more loyal and more worthy of retaining her position.

Yet many business and professional people report strong and thriving friendships that began at work. I'm only suggesting you weigh the potential risks (betrayal, gossip) against the potential gains (confiding in someone who understands).

Use these guidelines in choosing a confidant:

- *Ask yourself: What kind of response am I looking for?* Do I want constructive criticism? Sympathy? Advice? Do I want to think out loud or to vent anger and frustration?

  It may be helpful to get some critical appraisal of a problem from a co-worker. But with strongly controversial feelings, you may decide to talk to a family member who has no stake in the specifics of your complaints. If you are looking for sympathy, there is no place like home.

- *Remember that your feelings at the end of the day are often distorted;* they are intense and transient feelings. It may be safer to process your feelings alone, using techniques like Bathing with Nancy Reagan (See page 30) or Gaining Altitude (see page 68) before you share strong statements of feeling.

After a conversation, the other person will not see the transformation of your feelings; he or she will remember your feelings as you initially expressed them. Be sure to keep your confidant informed of any changes in your attitude.

You may also decide not to talk about work at all.

TECHNIQUE: When Silence Is Golden

Before you launch into your report of the day's events, you may first want to decide whether you want to relive your experiences.

Natalie, a social worker, states her preference: "By the time I get home, I have usually spent some time sorting out my feelings. If Bobby starts questioning me about work, I am forced to relive it all again."

You will need to convey your preference for silence with warmth and clarity. Like your homecoming greeting, your preferences should be stated in terms of your needs. You don't want your desire for silence to be interpreted as secrecy, a lack of trust or an unwillingness to express your feelings.

HE: How was your day?   SHE: A real killer, I'd like
                                  to forget it
                                  completely.

SHE: How was your day?   HE: Pretty hectic; I don't
                                  even want to *think*
                                  about it tonight.

But maybe you *do* want to talk about your day; you have strong feelings and opinions and you have decided to share them with a close friend or spouse. Rather than jumping in, try the next two techniques to preview your conversations about work.

"THOSE STORIES AT ELEVEN"

You are in the middle of watching a wonderful Joan Crawford movie. Suddenly the face of your local newscaster appears and proclaims, "Flooding on the Columbia, troops sent to Bulgaria. Those stories at eleven."

This preview informs you of the top stories of the day and lets you know what to expect when you tune in the news at eleven o'clock. You can borrow the newscaster's technique by offering a condensed version of your day and foreshadowing your intentions for further conversation.

Ralph, a physician, explains the need for foreshadowing the top stories: "I want the other person to give me a general status report of their needs before launching into a disaster they want to discuss. I hate to arrive at another crisis *immediately.*"

TECHNIQUE: The Condensed Version

The question "How was your day?" is a lot like the question "How are you?" Most people expect to get an automatic response of "fine" to either question.

Your best opening response to the question about your day is one that gives the questioner a *condensed* version of your answer and allows you to postpone the unexpurgated version for later in the conversation or later in the evening.

Your initial response should be succinct. Pick a sentence or two that summarizes your basic feelings and states your intentions.

SHE:	How was your day?	HE:	It's a long story, I'd like to get your opinion later.
HE:	How was your day?	SHE:	Really disappointing, I'm going to need a little tea and sympathy.
SHE:	How was your day?	HE:	Fantastic! I want to tell you what my client said about my presentation.

When you clarify your intentions, you can combat the problem of mind reading.

TECHNIQUE: Exchanging the Crystal Ball

At six o'clock, across the country, there is more mind reading taking place than at all the psychic fairs in Marin County. Listen to Ray as he predicts his wife's feelings. "When Janet comes in, I can take one look at her face and know that she had had a horrible day. I take my cue from her and offer to cancel any plans we have."

Some couples, like Ray and Janet, have developed elaborate mind-reading rituals that begin with a kiss at the front door and last all the way into the bedroom five hours later.

In this case, Ray knew that Janet, a travel agent, was worried about meeting her sales quota at work. He didn't want to put more pressure on her by asking her to make love during the week.

When they finally talked, Janet let Ray know that although she was under pressure at work, she was more worried about the fact that Ray seemed to have lost sexual interest in her.

Mind reading is an inaccurate, time-consuming trick. Instead of predicting the future, you will end up *creating* the future based on your own untested assumptions.

Janet could close off the possibility of mind reading by letting Ray know about her day and her wishes for the evening. She could exchange his crystal ball for some straightforward feelings and requests.

"I'm really beat; how would you feel about going to the movie tomorrow?"

"Today was the worst; I am looking forward to turning up the electric blanket and cuddling with you."

Don't make your initial feelings and intentions a topic of psychic research. Once you have clarified your intentions, you have opened up the possibility of talking about your day in greater detail.

When you "officially" begin to talk about your day, you will want to practice the art of editing.

THE ART OF EDITING: THE CUTTING ROOM FLOOR

All films and books are completed with the help of an editor— someone who makes decisions about what is essential to the main idea—and leaving the rest "on the cutting room floor." This section introduces five tools for editing the presentation of your day at work.

If you have done the "homework" in previous chapters, you will have a strong sense of your feelings about the day; but the feelings may not be in a form that another person can understand. If you are accustomed to greeting your family and friends with raw, unedited feelings about your day, you may, at first, feel uncomfortable leaving some of that day on the cutting room floor. You will feel like you are withholding vital information.

When you practice the art of editing, you'll find that your family and friends will become more attentive in listening to your feelings about work. This may be the ultimate benefit of editing: it leads to companionable listening.

Editing Tool #1:
Timing

I hope that you won't spend your whole evening, every evening, talking about work. Every couple and every friendship should determine the right time to talk about work and be able to set reasonable time limits.

My friend Hallie and I used to meet often after work. As we drove out to dinner, we would try to do all of our complaining about work before we arrived at the restaurant. Then we could relax over dinner and talk about love and movies and politics.

Before you launch into a long story about work, you'll want to practice two techniques that allow you to keep your eye on the clock.

TECHNIQUE: The Right Time

Your descriptions of work should be preceded by a brief environmental impact study. You need to take the other person's situation into account.

Is your mate in the middle of executing a complicated curry recipe? Maybe you should save your story until preparations are complete. Do you want his or her undivided attention? Maybe you could wait until the kids go to bed.

Choosing the right time depends on your awareness of your feelings and an understanding of the impact your statements can have. Don't set yourself up by announcing your intention to resign the minute you see your wife. She may need time alone to relax or to understand her own feelings about the day. You don't have to guess about the right time, you can simply ask: "I've got some problems at work, when would be a good time to talk?"

Next, practice the art of editing a long story.

TECHNIQUE: "To Make a Long Story Short . . ."

We used to have a joke in my family: Whenever anyone said, "to make a long story short," it really meant "stay tuned, this *is* a long story."

Walter, an airline pilot, explained his reaction to his wife's excess verbiage. "After a while, I stopped listening to Jane talk about her experiences. I kept thinking: get to the *point!*"

And from Jane: "I used to talk and talk to try to get Walter's attention. Now I look him directly in the eye and tell him a shortened version of my day—and he really listens."

Here are two guidelines for shortening your stories and lengthening your evenings.

- *Don't give an oral transcription of your conversations.*
  Only court reporters are responsible for a word-for-word account of the events of their day. Don't frame your story with "and then he said" and "then I said." These blow-by-blow descriptions are tedious and demanding conversations to follow.

- *Summarize the main points of an important conversation.*
  Use a critical quote only for emphasis.
  "So after chewing me out for fifteen minutes, he says, 'We really think you have a great potential here.'"

- *Don't build up to your main point by including irrelevant information.*
  Begin with your *conclusions* or the main point rather than leading up to it with dozens of tiny details.

Start by saying, "He did it again, he picked Ed to head up the campaign."

Don't begin with the whole story of how you got the news about Ed. Avoid stories that begin: "First Vince called both Ed and me into the office. I knew something was happening, since we didn't have anything important scheduled. Ed walks in, looking pretty pleased with himself. . . ."

If you really do have a long story, negotiate directly for the time to tell it. Tell your husband, "I am really upset. Can we take about thirty minutes to talk about it?"

If you bypass the time limits, don't just keep talking. Negotiate for more time: "It looks like we went over our limit. Can we talk for five more minutes to wrap it up?"

As you continue to talk, you may discover that your story needs a translation.

Editing Tool #2:
Translation

Every job and every profession has its abbreviations, codes and jargon. After eight hours of using work shorthand, you are likely to continue to use it at home. This jargon and in-house slang is the easiest material to edit out of your conversations about work.

Joan, a city planning manager, explained: "When I start using abbreviations from work, Chip gets that glassy-eyed look. Last week I started talking about SUP-DEV (supervisor development) and MFs (management forecasts) and I could tell that I had lost him completely."

You may decide to take the time to teach your family about some of the basic terminology in your field. If not, be prepared to translate your tasks and accomplishments into language that your loved ones can understand.

Follow three guidelines for translation:

- *Eliminate abbreviations that are unique to your job.*
  Court Psychologist: I had to interview the social worker from CPS and the diagnostic summary was heartbreaking.
  Translation: I had to interview the social worker from

Children's Protective Services and this family's history was a long, sad story.

- *Eliminate expressions you learned in graduate school.*
  Architect: The Land Use Department is requiring that we put the parking lot below grade. That will put our costs way over budget.
  Translation: The Land Use Department is requiring us to put the parking lot underground. That will cost our client $10,000 more.

- *Eliminate informal jargon that only your fellow professionals would understand.*
  Sales Representative: I don't seem to have any problem with prospecting; I just can't seem to move them to closing.
  Translation: I don't have a problem finding possible buyers; I just can't seem to get enough of them to sign on the dotted line.

Next, continue to edit your presentations with an eye to accuracy.

Editing Tool #3:
Accuracy

Dennis is a real estate broker who came to work and found that his secretary had called in sick. He had a stack of correspondence and contracts that needed to go out that day, so he cancelled most of his appointments and typed them himself.

He postponed all of his client meetings except for one lunch-hour meeting. At lunch, he accepted a $25,000 check as earnest money on a $500,000 house.

When Dennis came home, he offered his wife Karen the following version of his day:

I had the worst day! Evelyn called in sick and I had to do her typing myself. I was behind all day. I only had one client meeting and had to postpone the rest until later in the week.

I don't know why they don't get temporary help; they

never get temporary help. I don't know what I'll do if they don't get someone tomorrow. I just dread going in. . . .

Notice any missing information? It would be inaccurate to say that Dennis had a smooth day; he wouldn't want to omit the inconveniences and pressure of doing his own clerical work. But his description was inaccurate without the inclusion of the promise of the fat commission.

Try editing your accounts for accuracy by using this technique.

TECHNIQUE: When Accuracy Counts

As you think about summarizing your day, use the clichéd but useful formula of good/bad news. Ask yourself: "What is the worst thing that happened today? What is the best?" Be prepared to share both kinds of news.

Edit and delete words like *never* and *always*. These words have a strong effect on both the speaker and the listener. To you, things will sound worse than they are and you may elicit more sympathy than you need from a listener. Beware of crying wolf.

Consider the duration of the problem. Is this a permanent change or condition, or is it something that just happened today? Be sure to include a statement about how long the problem will last.

My favorite example of editing for accuracy comes from an attorney who called his wife after losing a costly litigation to collect fees from a client.

"Did anything good happen today?" his wife asked.
"*Not yet,*" he answered, hopefully.

Now let's explore an editing tool closely related to accuracy.

Editing Tool #4:
Shading

A technique called "Mount Vesuvius" was once very popular in therapeutic circles. Each person would take a turn and have ten minutes to spew angry and frustrated feelings toward family, bosses and co-workers.

I think the name Mount Vesuvius was rather apt in describing this technique—remember that the entire civilization of Pompeii was buried under the path of the volcano's molten lava.

When you are angry or frustrated about work, you want to share your feelings with someone, but you don't want to overwhelm them with your expression. Unedited venting of the Mount Vesuvius variety is not a form of sharing; it is a display of self-indulgence. And current research about anger suggests that unrestrained venting is not particularly therapeutic.

If you are alone (see Bathing with Nancy Reagan, page 30) or are stranded on a tropical island, you can enjoy some unrestrained venting. When you are with someone you love, you'll need to edit your feelings by shading both the positive and the negative experiences of your day.

Practice the editing principle of shading as you think about expressing angry feelings or gloating about your accomplishments.

TECHNIQUE: The Color Red

Jules Feiffer could have been thinking of the idea of shading when he said, "Artists can color the sky red because they know it is blue. Those of us who aren't artists must color things the way they really are or people might think that we are stupid."

When you are angry or irritated, you will be ready to color a blue sky red. The tendency is to express your feelings in the strongest possible terms.

Mick, an engineer, was trying to get some information about advanced graduate study and ran into an uncooperative department secretary. He described himself as being "furious" after this encounter. He groused, "I wonder if she ever got her high school diploma?"

Stress researchers have impressed us with the importance of mental labels. Most research suggests that stress is not the event (like Mick's encounter with the secretary) but the *label* assigned to the event ("I'm furious").

In this way, Mick's descriptions of his feelings might have influenced the way he felt: Was Mick really *furious*? What would have happened if he had decided to label his feelings in terms of being annoyed or just angry?

Remember, there is someone listening to you and taking your feelings seriously. Try to save that person unnecessary pain or concern for you. When you don't edit and shade, you may convince yourself and the listener that your situation is much worse than it needs to be.

You are entitled to strong feelings about events at work; the principle of shading means that you choose words that give your feelings an accurate shading. For every strong feeling, you have a number of choices about how to express yourself.

Try to avoid hyperbole and hysteria in your descriptions of work. Review some shadings of five basic feelings.

SHADES OF FEELING

	Mild	Moderate	Strong
1. ANGER	ANNOYED	ANGRY	FURIOUS
2. FEAR	CONCERNED	ANXIOUS	TERRIFIED
3. SADNESS	BLUE	DEPRESSED	MISERABLE
4. HURT	DISAPPOINTED	LET-DOWN	CRUSHED
5. SHAME	UNCOMFORTABLE	EMBARRASSED	HUMILIATED

Remember that sometimes you need to shade your success stories as carefully as your horror stories.

TECHNIQUE: The Shades of Success

You have every right to proclaim your accomplishments to dear friends and family. Any friend who isn't genuinely pleased with your good work should be dropped from your holiday shopping list.

Gloating about your success is another matter. Depending on the circumstances, you may decide to shade the presentation of your accomplishments. This is not like pretending to lose at tennis. You are not pretending that you didn't win; you are simply taking the other person's feelings into account.

Anna, a successful banker, explains the difference: "Within five minutes of getting into the car, Peter has told me about his day. If I have had a really great day and his day has been frustrating, I tell him about my triumph. *I just don't crow!*"

If you are hiding the *facts* of your success from your partner, your relationship is in peril. It is patronizing to withhold good news; your friends and lovers are not that fragile.

Yet, in many circumstances, you need to exercise self-control in your tall tales. Don't think of shading as losing at tennis; think of it as an act of kindness and consideration.

Neil gives an example: "I finally got promoted to supervisor and I was so high that I felt like I should advertise in the newspaper! It was hard *not* to gloat, since my friends were all in dead-end job situations and were feeling frustrated, though happy for me."

Few things are worse than a friend on a narcissistic binge. You have great fun seeing yourself in the brightest possible light (see Your Name in Lights, page 33), but the occasions when you can share that light should be influenced by your sensitivity to the other person's situation and adjusted accordingly.

Begin to share your good fortune with expressions like "I had some good news today," "Something terrific came my way" or "I have something wonderful to tell you"; but be prepared to edit the details when you learn of a friend's predicament.

For example, you have just been promoted and you are having lunch with a friend who is concerned about being laid off. It would be patronizing to withhold your triumph, but you could postpone the details. You don't need to dwell on your generous dental benefits and the view of the mountains from your new office. Tell her the details after her own crisis has passed, when she can appreciate the view.

Finally, you'll want to draw on your sense of humor to edit your day with a comic touch.

Editing Tool #5:
Humor

Chapter 2 explored the possibilities of seeing your day in a more humorous light. As you considered the lighter side of work, many of the "gory details" were left behind.

As a tool of editing, humor helps you to shape your telling of the day around comical interpretation of events. Although some events are truly devastating—and are not amenable to laughter—most daily pressures and mistakes can be reported with a humorous emphasis. You can be accurate in your description of the frustrations in your day; just let the other person know that in spite of what happened, you are inviting them to consider the incident with laughter.

Try three quick techniques to include humor in your descriptions of work.

TECHNIQUE: Introductions

Begin telling a work story with an introduction that promises laughter. Make sure that your nonverbal gestures match your words.

"The funniest thing happened to me today." (*smiling, chuckling*)

"You are going to *love* this story!" (*making direct eye contact, grinning*)

"Our sales meeting was something out of *Loony Tunes!*" (*smiling, eyebrows raised*)

These introductions help you to create the expectation of laughter. The principle is similar to the use of laughtracks; when you begin a story with humor, your laughter can be contagious.

TECHNIQUE: Share the Fantasy

If you have accomplished the feat of changing stressful situations into comic memories, share your perspectives as you talk about your day. You can display the results of techniques in Chapter 2.

If you draw cartoons, show them. If you have some good one-liners inspired by Carson or Rivers or Rickles, toss them out. If you began to see your day as fodder for a skit on *Candid Camera* or *Late Night with David Letterman*, share your comic fantasies.

Let the other person see the struggle you experienced as you tried to see humor in your day. "At first, I felt really angry about Emma. She always stares out of the window when I try to explain problems to her. Then, I started thinking how much she looked like Lily Tomlin's telephone operator, Ernestine. She even wears that cheap costume jewelry."

You can also try to imitate the difficult people in your day.

TECHNIQUE: Impersonations

If you decide to repeat a disturbing or irritating conversation from work, see if you can add some imitations of the other person. You don't have to be Rich Little to impersonate the gestures and language of clients and associates you work with every day.

Nonverbal gestures are the easiest to mock: Does she fiddle with a pencil behind her ear? Does he wrinkle his nose with disapproval or furrow his eyebrows in concentration?

If you are lucky, the person will have some kind of a regional accent or drawl that you can imitate. English and southern accents are easy to impersonate; so are New England Kennedy-style pronunciations.

You don't have to use an accent to repeat a colleague's frequent use of irritating figures of speech, like "up to speed," or to imitate a client's shrill, high-pitched laughter.

Your impersonations can help you to edit out some of the negative feelings and to share a light moment with someone at home.

But if the five editing tools haven't stopped you from presenting your day in the harshest light, try some emergency editing.

EMERGENCY EDITING

At the end of an exhausting day, you may not reach for your editing tools on the first draw. Many evenings you will forget to edit and belatedly notice yourself off on a tangent. You will suddenly find yourself in the middle of a long story sprinkled with jargon and overstated feelings and delivered in a flat, humorless tone.

Don't give up the evening as a lost cause. Catch yourself, apply your own brakes and put your words and deeds in reverse. Here is how your emergency application of the principle of accuracy sounds.

You are building up steam, using words like *always* and *never*; you are making a temporary situation sound interminable. You can stop yourself and offer: "You know, I think I am making this sound worse than it is. I know that the rush will subside after Christmas."

Now let's stop talking about work for a moment and listen to Hamlet's soliloquy.

HAMLET'S PROBLEM

Hamlet's chosen communication tool was the soliloquy. Shakespeare provided him with the material to make timeless statements about his personal and professional life. Yet his articulate conversations with himself didn't translate into meaningful discussions with others.

There is something about a soliloquy, no matter how eloquent, that discourages conversation. "To be or not to be?" was a rhetorical question, one that most listeners in the audience wouldn't touch.

As you travel home, editing your thoughts about work, you are engaged in a soliloquy about your day. When you come home to an audience of family and friends, you'll want to change your format from a monologue to a *dialogue*.

You can avoid Hamlet's problem and ask a series of questions to punctuate your soliloquy about work. You can break the silence and ask others to join you in a dialogue about your day.

TECHNIQUE: "That Is the Question . . ."

Follow three guidelines to initiate dialogue:

- *Notice the other person's nonverbal cues.*
  If his eyes become glassy or vacant, ask: "Am I going on too long?" If someone looks confused, ask: "Did I leave

something out?" or "You look confused, are you still with me?"

- *If you want advice, ask for it directly.*
  Don't expect the other person to know why you are telling a story. Be explicit about your intentions. You can say: "So what do you think he's up to?" or "How would you handle this?" or "What do you think; do you think I blew it?"

- *Use questions to punctuate your stories.*
  Tell him that he will appriciate the story because it will remind him of another person or situation. "Doesn't this sound like the stunts Alex used to pull? How did you ever get him under control?"

You are entitled to as much air time as you have negotiated. But if you want to move beyond Hamlet's style, you need to ask questions that will stimulate dialogue and a rich exchange of feelings after work.

YOUR TURN TO LISTEN

Talking about work creates a kind of paradox: Discussions about the office can prolong your feelings, but if you don't talk about work, the unspoken feelings may undermine your evening.

One couple solves the problem by devoting ten minutes to a game called "How was your day at school?" Each person gets five minutes to talk about their day and the rest of the evening is devoted to more playful or purposeful topics.

Once you have presented the edited version of your day, it will be your turn to listen.

Chapter 6
The Best Advice

SO LONG, FRANK LLOYD WRIGHT

I once toured Taliesin West, Frank Lloyd Wright's former residence/school in Arizona, where our tour guide relished telling a tale about the lady of the house.

It seems that one afternoon Frank was working in his studio and Mrs. Wright wandered in. He showed her a set of architectural drawings in progress, and she was pointedly critical of the decisions he had made.

Frank disagreed with her unsolicited critique and, shortly after, drove into town. During his absence, Mrs. Wright, who was not trained as an architect, went back to his studio and revised the drawings. Our guide smiled and informed us that Frank returned from town and found that her advice had been excellent; her revisions were just what the drawings needed!

Mrs. Wright's apocryphal intrusion is a perfect example of our most common response when we listen to loved ones talk about work: we give advice.

In this case, Mrs. Wright took one step further by actually

putting her advice into practice. Although her architect husband was ultimately pleased with the results, his initial irritation should not be overlooked.

Problems often occur when we offer advice before recognizing what the recipient feels or needs. Like Mrs. Wright, we assume that the way to demonstrate interest and concern is to give advice. But the best advice is offered by invitation only.

As a listener, your priority should be to recognize feelings before offering solutions. Consider five questions that frustrate, rather than encourage, the expression of feelings about work.

FIVE FREQUENT BUT FRUSTRATING QUESTIONS

Question #1:
"Why Don't You Quit?"

Carla, a financial analyst, had suddenly—inexplicably—become the target of a whispering campaign. When she walked into the conference room, conversation stopped. Colleagues who had been friendly offered only a cursory hello.

When she first noticed the problem, Carla was confused and hurt. She needed to sort out her feelings and try to map out a plan of action.

After several days, she sat down to explain her feelings to her husband, Gary. His response: "If it's really getting that bad, *why don't you quit?*"

His question, though asked out of a genuine love and concern, derailed the possibility for Carla to sort out her feelings. It served as the ultimate advice without exploring Carla's point of view. Gary's question marked the end of one conversation and the beginning of another.

Carla was suddenly forced to justify staying in a difficult job situation and was steered away from her feelings about the whispering campaign. Instead of pinpointing her feelings, she launched into an explanation of how hard it would be to find another job and how the loss of salary would cause financial problems.

Carla may eventually want to consider the possibility of leaving her job. But before she is ready to discuss such options, she needs to express her thoughts and feelings to Gary.

Gary's best advice should be preceded by recognizing Carla's strong feelings. As one hospital administrator explained, "I can't really solve work problems at home. I don't want advice, I don't want to debate; I want to talk about how I *feel*."

Later you'll practice the skill of paraphrasing feelings as a prelude to giving advice. The guiding principle is the order of your responses: feelings demand your first recognition.

Question #2:
"You're Not Going to Do/Say That, Are You?"

Most people who talk to you about work will not be aware of the five editing tools in the previous chapter. You may find yourself listening to some unedited venting of the Mount Vesuvius variety.

The rule of thumb is to take venting seriously but not *literally*. Todd, a dentist, describes the problem.

> Sometimes Marie takes my feelings *too* seriously. She'll pick me up in the car and I'll start complaining about my young associate. That arrogant SOB, I'm going to tell him. . . .
>
> Marie will get this look of panic on her face and ask me, *"You're not going to say that, are you?"*

As you listen to someone ventilate about work, you are providing companionship. A corporate vice-president explains why this is important. "There are such strong political implications of confiding in someone at work; I have to be so controlled at work. With George, I want to express my true feelings."

But you don't want to encourage unchecked venting. When you practice paraphrasing, you will find that recognizing feelings will *reduce* rather than increase the possibility that someone will actually carry out a verbal or physical threat at work.

Question #3:
"Do You Know What I'd Do?"

When you listen to someone express strong feelings about work, the most natural response is to associate their experience with something that happened to you. Your connection with your own experience may be a sincere attempt to understand, but your good intentions may be interpreted as a *failure* to understand.

When your husband is in the throes of a story about work, he feels that his situation is unique. If you listen and compare his situation with yours, he will think that you don't really understand.

Later in the conversation, your advice—based on a similar experience—may be helpful. But to begin, you need to validate his feelings. Responding with similar stories of your own, even in an attempt to show empathy, can often convey both one-upmanship and unsolicited advice.

HE: She did it again, she stared out her window during the entire meeting!

YOU: You think that's bad. I had a client once who did his paperwork *while* we were talking. I finally told him that if he was too busy to meet, we could re-schedule. *Do you know what I'd do?* I'd tell your client the same thing.

It might be helpful to share similar experiences, but wait for the person to ask for your perspective. Later we will talk about a role your advice can play in conversations about work.

For now, try to recognize feelings first.

Question #4:
"Why Do You Need to Talk About It?"

Jeanne, a television news director, is familiar with this question. "Art thinks I talk too much. He can't understand why I need to think and process my feelings out loud. He tends to work things out on his own, so he always asks me, '*Why do you need to talk about it?*'"

You may be a person like Art, who reviews and revises his feelings about the day on the freeway or on the tennis courts. When you come home, you cherish a respite from discussions about work and you resent another person's need to continue to talk about the day.

Questioning someone's need to talk about work will not reduce the number of words per minute. Your question is likely to produce even *more* talk. When Art questions the validity of Jeanne's feelings about work, she is likely to talk with increased intensity and to exaggerate her feelings. She will try to justify, in the strongest possible terms, why her feelings are worthy of discussion.

If you don't want to listen to an extended replay of someone's day, practice the art of paraphrasing. Once Art recognizes and validates Jeanne's feelings, she will feel relieved, and ready to move on to other topics and other activities.

Question #5:
"Why Do You Take It So Seriously?"

Your husband tells you, "I am really worried, I have only three weeks to create a complete promotional campaign for our client." You take one look at his pinched face and wish that he wouldn't take his work so seriously. You are tempted to say: "Oh, don't worry, you have time. After all, Handel wrote the whole *Messiah* in twenty-four days."

This attempt at humor may have a paradoxical effect: He may become even more serious as he attempts to convince you of the concerns you tried to laugh away.

Your first response as a listener can't be one of cheerful denial. If you smile and ask, *"Why do you take it so seriously?"* he will feel that you are trying to distract him or to deny that he has a problem. Instead, try recognizing his feelings with a simple restatement. You can say, "You are wondering if three weeks will be long enough to create a first-rate campaign."

When you paraphrase his feelings, you allow for the possibility for him to begin smiling—on his own time schedule.

Have you had enough of those frustrating conversations? Let's see if the act of recognizing feelings lives up to its buildup. Here is a closer look at the art of paraphrasing.

LEARNING FRENCH

Irwin Shaw's story "The Man Who Married a French Wife" makes a charming case for the importance of recognizing another person's world.

The narrator of the story is a man revisiting Paris with the French wife he married during World War II. During the long marriage, he has never taken the time to learn French or to understand his wife's heritage.

His wife introduces him to her former lover, a revolutionary. As the narrator learns of her past involvements in love and politics, he realizes how little time he has taken to understand her personal history or her point of view.

The story ends with him taking a thoughtful, hot bath. He asks, "I wonder if it is too late for me to learn French?"

It is seldom too late to learn the language that describes the experiences of a friend or lover. When you listen to talk about work, "learning French" means that you try to understand a person's experiences at work in their own terms.

I'd like to reintroduce the art of *paraphrasing* as a kind of translation check: You'll learn to restate what someone tells you, to check if you have understood their perspective about work. I say reintroduce because, unfortunately, the subtle art of paraphrasing became the fast food of psychology in the early 1970s.

Paraphrasing was then the cliché of every media psychologist and was often introduced with silly opening lines like "If I catch your meaning" or "I hear you saying." So annoying was this glib application of a subtle art that I used to threaten to fine my therapy trainees a nickel every time they used one of those openers!

In spite of the overexposure, paraphrasing remains the most effective communication skill in listening to talk about work. When you practice the art of paraphrasing as you listen to stories about work, you are attempting to restate what you have heard to indicate that you have understood both the situation and the feelings involved.

Paraphrasing—as the five frustrating questions indicate—is most useful as a *first* response to work talk. As a first response, it can set the climate for a comfortable conversation, help create a nonjudgmental atmosphere and reduce defensiveness.

When you paraphrase, you silently ask yourself two questions: *What is the situation?* and *How does she/he feel about the situation?*

When you attempt to understand a situation at work, you may be asked to follow a long story.

DETECTIVE'S WORK: THE LONG STORY

Most people have strong feelings about difficult personalities and complicated situations at work. Unfortunately, when friends and family talk about these situations, they may not have organized their thoughts. In many cases, it would take a detective to follow some of the stories you will hear about life at the office.

When listening to long stories, take advantage of an amusing fact: You can listen two to three times faster than someone else can talk. Theoretically, then, you could use your "extra time" to mentally outline and answer the question "What *is* the situation she/he is describing?"

For inspiration to answer the question, you can look to the work of television's most famous sleuths, one a detective and the other an attorney: Lieutenant Columbo, played memorably by Peter Falk, and Perry Mason, the alter ego of actor Raymond Burr.

TECHNIQUE: Columbo's Conclusions

By the time Lieutenant Columbo arrived on the scene in his rumpled raincoat, we already knew who the murderer was.

Virtually all of the episodes of *Columbo* began by showing and identifying the murderer. As viewers following the storyline, we knew the *conclusions* of Columbo's investigation before we knew the *facts* of the case.

Listening to some people talk about work is like watching an episode of *Columbo*. Like this physician talking about a series of job interviews, they will tell you their conclusions and then offer the details or facts of the story.

We finally decided to hire Dr. Riley. After interviewing fifteen candidates in three days, we narrowed it down to Riley and Dr. Edwards. Both had fine training and recommendations, but we felt that Riley's background in public relations would be good for the clinic.

People who offer the punch line—or the bottom line—first are the easiest to follow. Once they have stated their conclusions, you can do what Columbo did: Listen for the *facts* to fully understand the situation.

Other, more trying storytellers save the conclusions for *last*.

TECHNIQUE: Building the Case

If you watched *Perry Mason*, you never knew until the last five minutes, when Mason and D.A. Burger were nose to nose, who actually committed the murder.

Mason and Burger took turns in letting the details build. As viewers, we had to listen patiently to the minutiae of each case: the terms of the will and the condition of the body, the time the mail arrived and the time the suspect arrived.

We were rewarded for our perseverance when Perry Mason pointed to the murderer in court and restated how he had arrived at his conclusions. If you still didn't understand, the conclusions were reviewed in those famous post-trial lunches attended by Paul Drake and Della Street.

Listening to a friend talk about work can be as grueling as watching an episode of *Perry Mason*. You may have a loved one who relishes all of the detailed *facts* and saves the *conclusions* for last.

First we interviewed Dr. Morris from Dallas. He had a fine record, and it turns out he even went to medical school with one of the selection committee. . . . On Tuesday, we interviewed five more people. . . . Then we narrowed it down to Dr. Riley and Dr. Edwards. It seemed that they both had fine training and good recommendations. . . . But we felt that Riley's background in public relations would be good for the clinic. *We finally decided to hire Riley.*

If you can stand the suspense, keep track of the facts and listen carefully for the conclusions. If the wait becomes intolerable, you can say, "I'm getting lost. Can you tell me the punch line and then fill in the details?"

You can understand complicated work situations by mentally mapping the details and conclusions. You'll be ready to paraphrase once you've discovered the *feelings* that the situation evoked.

TECHNIQUE: Listening to Feelings

The physician who interviewed fifteen candidates and selected one will have some strong feelings about his involvement in the selection process. If you want to recognize and paraphrase his feelings, you will need to listen carefully.

He may feel relieved or tired; he may feel a sense of accomplishment or one of disappointment. Your goal as a listener is to understand how this situation has affected him.

When someone tells you a story about work, ask yourself: "*How does he/she really feel about this?*" You can review the same list of possibilities you used to connect your own feelings about work.

When you paraphrase, you don't want to overstate the feelings you have heard; you'll want to remember the shades of feeling that are charted on page 93.

NOT NECESSARILY A BULL'S EYE

After you have identified feelings and attached them to a specific situation, you'll be ready to paraphrase. Follow four steps when you want to recognize and restate someone's perspective about work.

- *Try to get inside of the person's frame of reference.*
  Ask yourself: "What is the basic feeling he/she is expressing? What is the situation or reason that evoked the feeling?"

- *Restate his or her feelings and reasons in your own words.*

- *Observe a cue from the other person that shows you have accurately restated his or her perspective.*

- *If not, try again.*

When you paraphrase, you fill in two blanks. A mental map of a paraphrasing statement would look like this: My friend feels
_____.

Example: A friend has just gotten the news that his mentor in the investment firm is taking a job in another city.

HE: After five years of getting Tom's best advice, I'm going to be left to fend for myself.
YOU: I can see that you are really going to feel a void when he leaves. (*Restating feeling.*) He's been one terrific guardian angel! (*Restating situation.*)
HE: You're right; sometimes I felt like he was the only person in the firm who really gave a damn about what happened to me. (*Confirms that your paraphrase was on target.*)

Your paraphrasing will not always hit the bull's eye, but your goal is to let the person know you are *trying* to understand. If you have misread a feeling, the other person can get you back on target.

Let's return to the friend who is losing a mentor.

YOU: It sounds like you are really *scared* about Tom leaving.
HE: Not *scared* really, maybe a little *anxious*. I don't know what that place will be like without Tom's helpful hints.

Don't worry about being right. You'll have many opportunities to communicate your willingness to understand.

But if you feel that you need more practice, try this game.

TECHNIQUE: "Do You Mean . . . ?"

Family therapist Virginia Satir suggests that paraphrasing can be practiced by playing a short game of questions.

Begin by sitting down and listening to a friend or family member tell you a story. Listen carefully and after they have finished, ask them a series of questions to restate basic feelings and reasons.

Keep asking questions that begin: "Do you mean that you felt

because _____?"

Keep asking questions until you get three yeses.

If paraphrasing doesn't seem to fit your style, remember that some ways of showing strong presence and recognition as a listener can be accomplished in few or no words at all.

TECHNIQUE: Winking, Blinking and Nodding

"When I tell Alan about my work, he doesn't say or do anything until I finish talking. I wish he would grunt or nod or *something*. I find myself getting distracted, wondering what he is thinking."

Nonverbal signs of encouragement are the essential acts of an empathic listener. Nodding, smiling, winking or leaning forward while a story is in progress are all ways of saying, "I'm listening; I'm following."

Some communication experts suggest that your facial expressions should mirror the feeling or tone of what the other person is saying. You can take your cue from the person talking to you: If she is laughing, you can smile; if he is frowning, you can nod and frown slightly or wrinkle your nose.

You can add small verbal phrases of encouragement to remind the person of your interest. Little phrases like "um-hmm," "go on" and "I see" are short but sweet signs to the person seeking your undivided attention.

These nonverbal gestures and brief encouragements indicate your willingness to withhold judgment and recognize the person's immediate feelings before offering your advice.

THE BEST ADVICE

When you recognize the feelings of family and friends through encouragement and paraphrase, you will have established a climate for mutual problem-solving. In this atmosphere, the best advice is offered by invitation only.

Practice two techniques to initiate the process of moving beyond feelings about work to the solution of work-related problems.

TECHNIQUE: Brainstorming

A favorite technique of organizational consultants, brainstorming describes a process in which participants suggest every possible solution to a problem without evaluating each suggestion. The process allows a group to think out loud and to consider unconventional possibilities in a safe atmosphere.

Brainstorming can initiate the process of problem-solving in conversations about work. You can begin with a simple question: *"Have you thought about your options?"*

This technique is most effective when you have recognized the feelings involved. Carla, the financial analyst concerned with office whispering is a case in point.

Her husband, Gary, listened to her story and offered her an immediate option: he suggested that she quit. His alternative was to recognize and paraphrase Carla's feelings of confusion and hurt. Once he had established his understanding of her perspective, he might have asked about her options.

Rather than suggesting ideas for an option, let the other person brainstorm by listing any possibilities that come to his or her mind. As a listener, you should withhold judgment and simply restate the options as you continue to explore possibilities.

Carla and Gary's brainstorming session could have sounded like this:

> GARY: It all sounds so confusing—like you don't really have a clue about how this whispering got started. *(Paraphrasing.)*

CARLA: Yeah, I'm completely stumped. (*Confirms his paraphrase was accurate.*)

GARY: Have you had a chance to think about your options for getting to the bottom of this? (*Doesn't demand answers or offer advice; just opens the discussion.*)

CARLA: I was thinking about asking Burt; he has always been honest with me. But if *he* is involved in the problem, I wouldn't want to give him any ammunition. . . . (*States an option and her own objection.*)

GARY: So Burt is a possibility, but you're not even sure that you trust him. (*Restates option and objection; doesn't evaluate or give advice.*)

If Carla and Gary continue to brainstorm, Carla will have the opportunity to think out loud with the benefit of Gary's empathic companionship. She is likely to arrive at a plan of action as a result of their discussion.

Before the discussion ends, Carla may ask Gary for his advice. Advising, when preceded by paraphrasing and brainstorming, can be a marvelous way to communicate that you have been listening.

Once again, the important factor is that you have recognized feelings first and that your advice has been requested.

Let's reconsider the Taliesin West tall tale about Frank Lloyd Wright in terms of the technique of advice by consent.

TECHNIQUE: The Wrights Revisited

Mrs. Wright could have offered her famous advice in a less intrusive manner. She could have asked her architect husband a simple question: "*Do you want my opinion?*"

Let's say that the drawings in question were for a residence to be built on ocean-front property in California, and that Mrs. Wright thought that the living room facing the ocean didn't have enough windows.

If Mr. Wright had invited her critique, she could have followed three rules for giving advice with consent.

1. *Acknowledge your limitations. Recognize the fact that you are offering an opinion that lacks the background of and experience in the other person's field.*

MRS. W: I know I'm not an architect, but if I were sitting in that living room, I would want more windows and more of an ocean view.

2. *Once you have stated your opinion, don't press your point. If the other person disagrees, don't debate; paraphrase their point of view.*

MR. W: Yes, but in the evening after the sun goes down, you would look out and see a big, dark and blank space. You couldn't see the ocean. I decided to put this fireplace on the ocean wall to provide a warm focus in the evening.

MRS. W: So you have thought about the windows, but decided that it was more important to reduce the dark outlook.

3. *Don't become invested in your opinion or advice. Offer your perspective and indicate your interest in the other person's decision.*

MRS. W: It is an interesting problem. I'd love to see the rest of the drawings when you finish.

Endless conversations about work can create the illusion of extending the workday into the night. If you can enjoy satisfying, limited conversations about work, you'll be able to enjoy the hours after work.

Part
THREE

AFTER HOURS

Chapter 7

From Work to Love

THE COMMON WISDOM

Picture yourself coming home, tired, struggling to unwind from the problems of the day. You are looking forward to fixing an early dinner and chatting with your partner in front of the fire.

As you open the door, you see that all of the lights are out except in your bedroom. You enter the bedroom and find your husband or wife in bed, drinking champagne. With a smile of unmistakable intention he or she says, "Welcome home, darling."

This scenario has been the common wisdom about love after work. With endless variations suggested by authors and advertisers, we are advised to greet each other in everything from a negligee or jockey shorts to Saran Wrap.

My quarrel with this advice is not in the choice of attire but in the emphasis on sex rather than intimacy at the end of the working day. A costumed greeting is a poor substitute for true intimacy—that rare combination of passion, affection and companionship.

The transition from work to love is celebrated in the famous toast "Here's looking at *you*." Intimacy demands that you turn your attention away from yourself and focus on the loving presence of your partner.

This transition requires time and patience. From the moment you arrive, you will be struggling to protect your time together from the problems of your day at work.

FROM SHOP TALK TO SWEET TALK

Talking about and listening to feelings about work are the foundation of a cozy evening at home. When you can acknowledge anger, disappointment and fears, you become vulnerable, more open to your sexual feelings.

As you recognize the feelings of your mate, you indicate your willingness to become a receptive, empathic partner.

It takes an enormous amount of energy to withhold and hide feelings about work, and the feelings rarely stay hidden. Consider two scenarios where feelings about work appear in a disguised form. In each case, they interfere with the growth of trust and comfort in the relationship.

Hidden Failures

I will never forget my lunch with Ken, an attorney whose practice had failed to prosper. He was exhausted, depressed and talked about declaring bankruptcy.

"How does Ellen feel about all this?" I asked. Ken shifted in his chair and answered, "She doesn't know."

Nor can I forget a spectacular shouting match between Ken and Ellen on the balcony of their rented apartment on Martha's Vineyard. "I hate you," screamed Ken, within earshot of hundreds of people on the beach.

Marriage is not an arena for keeping up a good front. Ken may have hidden his business failures from his legal colleagues, but he should have confided them to his wife.

Instead, he borrowed money, juggled funds and became hopelessly overextended on his credit cards. He tried "hinting" to Ellen, and eventually resented her for "not guessing."

Talking about fears and failures allows you to express a vulnerability that is *the* prerequisite for intimacy.

Ken could have shared his financial burdens with Ellen. When he chose to hide his failures, he created a wall of resentment, and both of them lost the opportunity to deepen their relationship during the difficult times.

Frozen Anger

Mary Anne came home after finding out that one of her employees had gone over her head to reverse a decision she had made. She was determined not to ruin the evening by talking about it. Her husband, Daniel, asked about her day, and she offered a vague description.

As the evening continued, Mary Anne found herself getting into a series of mini-battles with Dan: why hadn't he fed the cats, why did they *have* to visit his parents this weekend. When they got into bed and Dan moved closer, she said, angrily, "I'm just not in the mood. Couldn't you tell?"

Dan began a gentle, probing conversation with Mary Anne and they were able to connect the source of her anger. By the time they finished talking, they were too tired to make love, but they fell asleep with their arms around each other.

When you state your feelings of anger or frustration about work, you clear the path for more affectionate and sexual expression.

After all of your careful and caring conversations about work, you'll be ready to change the subject. The transition from work to love can be graced by a rich exchange of feelings and appreciations.

TECHNIQUE: The Next Subject

Sandra and David work together in a hospital laboratory, doing ground-breaking scientific research. "My husband could talk about work constantly if I didn't stop him," said Sandra. "One night, I was fixing dinner and he began to talk to me about the results of the day's tests. I got very angry and told him, 'You must stop this. I cannot talk about science twenty-four hours a day.'"

She reports that they now have imposed a rule of a brief work-related conversation and then a change of subject. "We really enjoy talking about the people we know, what they are doing—what makes them tick."

Mona and John moved to Los Angeles to accept high-pressure jobs in the entertainment business. In their first months, they talked about work throughout dinner every night. After six months, they set some limits.

They put aside fifteen minutes to debrief news about "the business" and then, says Mona, "We like to talk about the kind of life we are living, whether we want to have children or buy a house or whether our values have changed since we moved here."

Talking about work can be a symptom of work stress or a sign of a relationship without shared interests. Sometimes talk about work is a means of escaping silence or boredom.

Make a practice of changing the subject. If you and your partner are in a rut of talking about work, try another topic. Some possibilities are: presidential politics, family (yours, mine and ours), good news about friends, the book or magazine article you are reading, whether to vacation in Mexico, see Woody Allen's latest movie, buy a home computer, join the Sierra Club, or . . .

As you shift the focus away from your concern about work, you'll be able to express your appreciation of each other. Compliments and thank-you notes can be a delightful change of subject.

TECHNIQUE: "Let Me Count the Ways"

Time at home provides the opportunity to look at your partner in emotional, appreciative terms. You don't have to be a poet to "count the ways" in which your partner delights you. But you may have difficulty translating your feelings of appreciation into words.

In your search for a fitting compliment, ask yourself:

- If you ran into a friend who hadn't seen you in ten years and had never met your partner, how would you describe him or her?
- If you wrote a profile of your partner as a most unforgettable character, what qualities would you emphasize?

As you begin to discover the depth of your appreciation for your partner, develop the habit of sharing your sweet and loving feelings. The key is to be specific. Rather than saying, "You are really generous," say: "I love watching your face light up when you pick up the tab for dinner with friends."

Practice accepting compliments: When your wife tells you how generous you are, stifle your impulse to deny it. Catch yourself, smile and reply, "What a nice thing to say."

TECHNIQUE: Thank-You Notes

"Thank you" can be two of the sweetest words at the end of the day. Each one of us thrives on the feeling of being appreciated, and intimates are well advised to practice the art of sending verbal thank-you notes.

Develop the habit of appreciating your partner's thoughtful words and deeds.

- *Be specific; mention time and place.*
  Don't say: "You are really good to me." Instead, try: "Last night, when you talked to me about my supervisor, you really helped me figure out what to do. Thanks for listening to me rattle on and on about it."

- *Stay current.*
  Try to mention your appreciation within twenty-four hours. Thank-yous lose their punch over time. "That was a wonderful dinner you planned for my mother tonight" has more appeal than "I have been meaning to thank you for the way you made Mom's birthday so special last week. . . ."

You'll also want to talk about plans for your time after work. To do this, be ready to eliminate the task orientation that motivates you during the workday.

FROM PURPOSEFUL TO PLAYFUL

You race through the workday, returning phone calls, dictating letters and meeting with colleagues, clients, students or patients. You set priorities, make decisions and solve problems. Efficiency is the greatest good during business hours. After work, a sense of purpose can reduce spontaneity.

The Management Mode

When you make the transition from work to love, the task orientation of the day can diminish the prospects of a playful or sexy time at home.

Claudia and Tim, a busy professional couple, realized that they were depriving themselves of time off from work. Claudia explained, "On Saturday morning, we'd start with our list: rake leaves, fix storm windows, do laundry, shop for groceries. . . . We used to make love in the afternoons; now we are too efficient. We get into our 'management mode' and spend the day finishing tasks. We don't even get *near* the bedroom."

It is important to turn off the work habit of overscheduling time. Intimacy is established at a slower, more spontaneous pace. You'll need to postpone the sense of purpose that motivates you during working hours.

You might start by changing your name.

TECHNIQUE: "Who's Pinkie?"

In the movie *Adam's Rib*, Katharine Hepburn and Spencer Tracy are the glamorous epitome of a two-career couple. This relationship of two attorneys meshes beautifully until the day they face each other in court.

In a hilarious courtroom scene, they confound the judge by referring to each other by a private nickname:

"It wasn't that way at all, Pinkie," says Hepburn for the defense.
"That's what *you* think, Pinkie," says Tracy for the prosecution.
"Who's Pinkie?" asks the judge.

Private nicknames are the way that many couples draw the line between professional and intimate conversations. One physician is Dr. Matthews by day, and "Gumby" at night. His wife calls him Gumby because he is tall, slim and very limber in bed!

Nicknames are the result of the private conversations and shared experiences of a couple. Pet names should be silly, sexy and fun. They are a definite reminder that you have come home from work. But you may need more than a reminder.

The Overplanned Vacation

Lisa and Patrick looked forward to their spring trip to Italy all winter. They had booked hotels, ground tours and opera tickets months in advance.

Somewhere between Venice and Florence, they began to feel exhausted. The itinerary they had so carefully planned and booked in advance was interfering with their enjoyment of each other. They would set their alarm, rise early and tackle the second floor of the Uffizi Gallery. As each evening arrived, they would drag themselves to sit through a prebooked concert or play and then return to the hotel, too tired to make love.

They finally decided to cancel some of their plans and take a lesson from their Italian hosts, a people famous for their capacity to savor the sights, sounds and smells all around them.

At work, we are oriented toward a linear progression of events: If we finish A, we can proceed to B. Playful, sensual time has no goal other than the enjoyment of all of your senses.

TECHNIQUE: **Smell the Pizza**

In most jobs, we try to shut out the stimulation of our senses so that we can concentrate; we receive most information through our eyes and ears. Intimate relationships thrive on awakening the neglected senses of touch and taste and smell.

On your way home from work, make an effort to reconnect with rich sensory experiences: Walk past an Italian restaurant and smell the pizza. Stop at a fruit stand and bite into a crisp, fragrant apple; feel your silk slip brush against your legs; blink the raindrops from your eyelashes.

Jean Houston, author of *The Possible Human*, asked a group of her friends to list their most pleasurable sensory experiences. You might want to join your partner in summoning forgotten sensory delights.

- The hot sand under your feet on the beach.
- The sight of Bob Dylan's shockingly blue eyes seen through binoculars during a concert.
- A ride through a light snowfall with your convertible top down.
- The cologne you wore in high school.
- A chocolate soda with chocolate ice cream.

Sweet, confiding conversation and sensory enjoyment allow you to anticipate the pleasure of making love after work—that is, if you can keep your preoccupation with goals out of the bedroom.

FROM PRESSURE TO PLEASURE

Making love can be the celebration, if not the focus, of genuine intimacy. It is also, as one attorney admits, "the first thing to go" when the pressures of work add up.

The problems of fatigue, unfinished business and self-absorption stand in the way of intimacy and arousal. So, in a very real sense, you can consider every technique and every suggestion in this book as an act of foreplay.

When you practice techniques to review, and share your feelings about work, you have taken the first steps in becoming emotionally available. If you can switch from a task orientation to a sensual and playful focus, you remove another obstacle to intimacy.

The final obstacle involves removing the concern with performance from your experience of sexual love.

Sex by Objectives

It makes good business sense to set a series of professional objectives for yourself and for the people you manage. It is pure madness to be concerned with your goals and performance in bed.

When you say, "I'm too tired," you may be speaking in code. You may really mean that you're too tired to have multiple orgasms or to search for your G-spot. You might enjoy cuddling or a less than transcendent sexual encounter; but you have set other goals for yourself.

You might actually feel that orgasms are highly overrated at the end of an exhausting day, that you would enjoy sharing other sexual play, but you think that your partner has other goals in mind.

The joy of a sexual relationship after work is sharing warm moments together, and you can plan to share some kind of sexual experience together every day. You can enjoy moments of fantasy and touch that allow you to stay connected to each other's sexual self.

I won't even use the word *technique* in this section; the key is to experience sexual play that is not oriented toward specific goals. The approaches that follow can initiate delightful sexual encounters after work.

You can enjoy them with—or without—orgasm.

UNDRESS FOR SUCCESS

Dressed in jeans and crew-neck sweaters, Claudia and Tim sat in my office talking about their difficulties in leaving behind the "management mode" they both carried home from work.

Claudia said she had the most trouble leaving her goals behind. She paused thoughtfully, and I found myself wondering about the clothes she wore to work. I asked her to describe her work clothes to Tim. How did she feel when she wore them?

"I always wear a dark suit with a high-collared blouse, plain pumps and very little jewelry; I work hard at hiding any hint of sexiness. When I come home, I feel very tight and buttoned down, not very responsive."

The act of "turning in her suit" had real significance for Claudia, and she began to use the change of clothes as a means of creating a different picture of herself after work. She and Tim began also to plan deliberate rituals, like enjoying a glass of wine together to create a more intimate homecoming.

The act of changing clothes is an important ritual for most people at the end of the day. For many couples, the experience of undressing together becomes an integral part of sexual play.

One couple occasionally plays strip poker before drifting off to sleep; another begins every heart-to-heart talk by taking off their clothes. Other couples take long soapy showers together.

TEENAGE THRILLS

Ron, a stockbroker, confided in me: "When my wife and I were first dating, we used to spend these long evenings just kissing and holding each other. It was wonderful. I felt just like a teenager!"

He wistfully concluded, "Now we just jump straight into bed."

Remember back seats and drive-in movies and the front porch? Those make-out sessions seemed to last for hours, with the promise that "maybe next time. . . ."

You can enjoy the thrills of a teenager's anticipation of sex. Even when you feel "too tired" to make love, you can still enjoy some long sweet kisses and lingering caresses.

"Next time" will arrive soon enough.

FANTASYLAND

Walt Disney can't be your guide to this approach, but shared (not acted upon) fantasies can be an alternative for exhausted participants. You can stimulate your imaginations, if not your bodies.

- *Think about a change in location.*
  "I'd like to be sitting in a cafe in Paris with you, on the way to our tiny room on the rue des Écoles."

- *Think about an unexpected encounter.*
  "What if you walked into my office during lunch, and we made love before anyone returned?"

- *Share memories of your greatest hits.*
  "Remember the night of Nancy's wedding?"

- *Make promises you can keep.*
  "Let's sleep in tomorrow and have breakfast in bed."

James Thurber summed up the essence of pure enjoyment of sexual feelings *without* objectives when he said: "I love the idea of there being two sexes, don't you?"

A QUESTION OF INTIMACY

Denise, a very composed physician, slid into the chair next to mine at a clinic meeting. In the middle of a rather mild conversation she blurted: "Paul and I have been so busy, we just haven't made love in over a month!"

The pressures and demands of work can contribute to the escalation of a situation like Denise's. Each partner comes home fatigued, self-absorbed and irritable; these are not the feelings that contribute to shared intimacy after work.

The approaches in this chapter can offer delightful options for intimate encounters. But if you begin to feel that even these playful options are a chore, there may be more to your avoidance of intimate contacts than your tyrannical boss.

Concerns about work can become a cover for unspoken anger or anxiety about the relationship itself. If you sense this pattern, sit down with your partner and explore your feelings together.

Begin by expressing your feelings about the loss of intimate times together. Ask your partner's help in uncovering anger, resentment or anxiety in your relationship. Are either of you upset about children, in-laws, housework, money, lack of appreciation, the division of labor or power in the relationship?

Are unspoken feelings clouding your time together and causing you to use work as a smokescreen? Question each other tenderly about work and about feelings in your relationship that may be keeping you from enjoying the transition from work to love.

The next chapter explores the role of work in undermining a different kind of intimacy—the closeness between friends.

Chapter 8
Friendship: Business or Pleasure?

FRIENDSHIP: A MOVEABLE FEAST?

In the winter of 1924, Harold Loeb invited Ernest and Hadley Hemingway to a lobster dinner at the Negré de Toulouse in Paris. Loeb couldn't have imagined that two years later he would be humiliated when his friends recognized him as a model for the passive Robert Cohn in *The Sun Also Rises*.

Hemingway's biographer Carlos Baker reports that Hemingway developed quite a reputation for using his friends as models for the characters in his novels. Loeb was neither the first, nor the last, to be the subject of Hemingway's devastating caricatures.

It could be argued that all writers transform their relationships within their work. But Hemingway was known for viewing his friendships as fair game.

My queasiness with Hemingway's betrayal of his "cafe society" extends to other working professionals who contaminate their friendships with business styles and agendas.

Many professionals allow their friendships to walk a thin line

127

between business and pleasure. Friendship becomes yet another arena in which to practice skills that are productive in professional life but destructive to the growth of intimate relationships.

Friendship offers a precious opportunity to remove yourself from the competitive professional world. If you approach friendship with a business agenda, you lose the chance to cultivate a life separate from work. In this chapter you will recognize three aspects of professional savvy that can undermine the growth of loving relationships.

SOME FRIENDLY QUESTIONS

When you invite two couples for dinner, do you:
   a. Buy two more place settings from your wedding pattern?
   b. Start speedreading through Julia Child?
   c. Call a maid?
   d. Ask your wife or husband not to call you "Chubby" during dinner?

You are having dinner with a friend for the first time in three months. Do you:
   a. Spend the whole evening talking about how busy you are?
   b. Cancel a date at the last minute for dinner with a client?
   c. Talk about time you spent with other friends?
   d. Make a point of telling about how hard you tried to fit him or her in?

For your daughter's wedding, would you:
   a. Invite fifty of your clients?
   b. Bring an extra supply of business cards?
   c. Dance with the boss's wife?
   d. Refuse to try break dancing with your nephew?

If you answered "yes" to any of the choices, you have experienced the intrusion of your business style into precious time with friends. Consider the possibilities for protecting close friendships from your professional expertise.

MAKING AN IMPRESSION: A TWENTY-FOUR-HOUR JOB

The ability to create a good impression is the foundation of all successful business relationships. During the course of the work week, we all struggle to project a polished, professional profile in the face of strong competition from colleagues.

The effort to achieve and maintain a good impression often persists after work. When this happens, you deprive yourself of the ultimate pleasure of intimacy: the chance to be relaxed, genuine and cooperative.

If you are scrambling to "look good," you won't have the chance to be silly, to tell bad jokes or to tarnish your cool, professional veneer. You won't be cultivating friends that you can call at three in the morning.

If you enter friendships determined to present a competitive business profile, you won't risk talking about your disappointments and your dreams. To open up possibilities for genuine intimacy, you need to abandon your desire to impress your friends.

Impression #1: Cleaning Up for Company

Many working people refuse to invite friends into their homes because "the house is a mess" or "we haven't had time to re-cover the sofa, buy six wine goblets, paint the dining room, get guest towels for the bathroom or. . . ."

Those who focus on making an impression at home have forgotten the purpose of extending an invitation. Remember, your friends come for the pleasure of your company, not to inspect the glasses for spots. The intimacy of your kitchen or dining room table adds a dimension of enjoyment that is unavailable in even the most intimate of restaurants.

If your real purpose is to enjoy your friends, you don't need the services of a maid or an interior decorator before extending an invitation. Practice asking yourself an important question.

TECHNIQUE: "What's a Few Crumbs Among Friends?"

Rachelle, a charming university official, reminds herself of the importance of friendship and the triviality of "cleaning up for company." "I am a single parent with two kids. Our house stays clean for about five minutes at a time. When I get concerned about visiting friends, I ask myself, 'So, what's a few crumbs among friends?'"

Impression #2:
Cooking for Company

Formal dinner parties may be appropriate for entertaining heads of state and chairmen of corporations. But do you really want friendships that depend on your dexterity in stuffing a Cornish game hen?

You say no, but why does the prospect of inviting friends to dinner initiate the frenzied purchase of truffles, fresh basil and designer pasta?

When the "company" is close friends, the idea is to create a relaxed atmosphere for an informal evening. You can't help others feel at ease if you are concentrating on whether or not the walnut sauce has thickened.

Elaborate menus can impair spontaneity in conversations. How many times have you had a dinner party where you spent the evening like a jack-in-the-box, jumping up every three minutes to check on the next course?

Remember, the priority of the evening should be conversation, not cuisine. After years of cooking for company, I made an agreement with a friend.

TECHNIQUE: Gourmet Armistice

One day at lunch I was talking to my friend Laura about how we had stopped inviting each other to dinner. And I decided to take the plunge.

I said: "I think one reason we rarely invite each other is because we feel we have to make something special for dinner. By now, we know that all four of us are good cooks; what would happen if we agreed on *no more rack of lamb?*"

We laughed and talked about how we could plan for more casual, less elaborate evenings together. We freed each other from the urge to cook for company by agreeing to some new patterns for spending time together.

Try some of these possibilities to plan for your own gourmet armistice.

- When a friend asks, "Can I bring anything?," answer "Yes, how about dessert?" Potluck dinners don't mean you don't have the money to feed your friends; they allow you to share time together.
- Invite friends to help you prepare a complicated recipe. Spend the evening in the kitchen, drinking wine and exploring the mysteries of Cantonese cooking.
- Don't feel that everything must be ready before your friends ring the bell. Invite them into the kitchen and enjoy the conversation while you prepare dinner.
- Give up the idea that you must cook everything yourself. Buying breads, desserts and salads can allow you to cut your preparation time in half and to feel freer to invite guests at the last minute. Ask yourself: Will the evening really be less festive if I buy, rather than make, a Black Forest cake?

Other friends can vouch for the success of their armistices. Michelle describes the essence of *enjoying*, rather than cooking for, company. "With everyone's crazy schedules, David and I treasure our time with Bill and Anna. We are thrilled to grab a pizza, bring it over to our house and talk, talk, talk."

The exception is for those who find cooking a form of relaxation. If chopping garlic and separating egg whites are the acts of a soothing, relaxing hobby, you won't feel the pressures of the "bake-off" scenario.

If you are one of those rare people who delights in sharing a newfound, inexpensive Chardonnay with friends—and can talk about it without stagy affect—continue to share your discoveries.

Just examine your motives carefully: If you are cooking and pouring to impress your friends, you are working too hard. Get out of the kitchen and get involved with your guests.

Impression #3:
"We Couldn't Be Happier"

When you see your friend David kiss the tip of his wife Sharon's nose, your first thought may be: "I wonder if they make love more often than we do" or "Do *we* seem as happy/sexy as they do?"

It takes two to compete in this round; the goal is to impress your friends that you and your partner are the happiest couple in your circle. Have you been spending time with friends fondling your spouse, displaying your anniversary presents or swearing that you never argue about household chores?

When you waste time with friends demonstrating your own happiness, you lose the opportunity to enjoy the warmth, trust and silliness that couples can share. Dinner parties, picnics and weekends at the beach can become a series of dance contests. All you would need is Dick Clark appearing from behind the bandstand to hold his hand over your head and say: "Let's hear it for Couple Number 1. . . ."

If your time with other couples is colored by competitive thoughts and observations, try to shift your thoughts into a less competitive gear.

TECHNIQUE: Second Thoughts

Maybe you will always have a first impulse to present your relationship in the best possible light. But your *second* thoughts can be less competitive.

When you see David kiss Sharon's nose, stop yourself from applying your lips directly to *your* partner's nose. Try to substitute a second set of less comparative thoughts:

"They seem happy; that's great."

"Slow down; this isn't *The Newlywed Game*."

"I enjoy having friends who are happy together."

When you catch yourself competing with close friends, refuse to compete. Focus your thoughts in another direction.

Impression #4:
Business Is Great!

In the movie *Fun With Dick and Jane*, we see a recently fired executive (George Segal) trying to impress a potential employer at dinner. The dinner, prepared by his wife (Jane Fonda), is expensive and elegant. The point of the dinner is to hide the couple's desperation and to impress the employer with Dick's casual affluence. Meanwhile, during dinner, landscape contractors are outside removing trees and shrubs that the couple can't pay for.

It may be important to convince potential employers and clients that business is good. With friends, however, this charade will deprive you of warmth and support during difficult times. You need to have at least one close friend to whom you can say, "Business is terrible. I'm living on hot dogs and macaroni until the first of the month."

The struggle to appear successful during the work week can become an exhausting deception with close friends. Examine your motives carefully. Does the desire to compete with close friends push you to give the impression that business is great?

TECHNIQUE: The Real Story

I agree that it would be self-destructive to broadcast the details of your floundering business or career. But it is also destructive to keep the reality of your struggles to yourself.

Signs of competition during bad times include agreeing to meals, vacations, tickets and events you can't afford. You'd rather be hounded by your credit card company than admit that you can't afford to participate.

Hard times are lonely and scary. Don't deepen the pain by pretending. If you pretend as a way of maintaining an impression or competing with friends, you will feel a chilling sense of isolation.

Tell at least one friend the real story about your professional life. Allow a friend to demonstrate his or her concern and belief in you. You'll find that your friendships don't depend on your ability to rent a condo in Aspen during Christmas.

Refuse to participate in social gatherings you can't afford. Tell friends, "I'm on a lean and mean budget this month, so the Four Seasons is out."

Try to protect friendships from your skills in impression management and your skills in managing time.

TIME MANAGEMENT: "BUSIER THAN THOU"

Time management is number one on the hit parade of corporate training classes. As a result, millions of working people walk through the day muttering about the need to "prioritize."

Your ability to establish priorities and to manage your time on the job may be a key element in your successful career or business. When your preoccupation with time and efficiency extends to the hours after work, you can destroy the spontaneity and delight of time with friends.

Time with friends offers a different experience of time than the priorities you set on the job do. Your friends will not be impressed with how busy you are, and they don't want to be "managed."

THE WHITE RABBIT

Your profile as a friend may bear a strong resemblance to Alice's tour guide in Wonderland. When you talk to friends on the phone, you are "just on your way out." You can't get together next week because you have been "working too hard." You may not actually say it, but your friends have the distinct impression that you are always "late, late, for a very important date."

I am still cringing from my latest stumble into the rabbit hole, and I appreciate my friend Ralph for pointing it out to me. We had plans for dinner when my sister unexpectedly flew in from Los Angeles. Instead of simply cancelling our dinner plans, I said: "We could reschedule, but then I'd be out every night this week." Ralph told me later, "You know, I didn't mind you changing plans because of your sister, but when you told me about your whole *schedule*, I felt pretty unimportant."

Like Ralph, your friends may feel like clients that you are trying to "fit in." Or you may have cultivated the bad habit of cancelling dates with friends to accommodate the last-minute requests of bosses or business associates.

It is important to spend playful time with friends that is free from the efficient management of your time. Consider these possibilities for creating and protecting special times for your friendships.

- Cultivate the habit of thinking of personal dates as carrying the same kind of commitment as business dates.
- Stop talking about how busy you are or where you have to go on Monday.
- Plan to occasionally say no to the last-minute requests of your boss and to keep your date with a friend.
- Don't use the expressions *fit you in* or *booked* when making a date with a friend.

Friendships cannot flourish when intimates foster the value of staying "busier than thou." You need to separate and protect special time for your friends.

It is also essential to keep your circle of friends at a safe distance from your network of professional associates.

THE DARKER SIDE OF NETWORKING

Your network of business contacts is the foundation of a lifelong career plan. As you cultivate the professional habit of "high visibility," you may begin to wonder where your business network ends and your friendships begin.

Diana, a consultant I admire, describes the problem. "I was making up the guest list for my husband's birthday party and I noticed that I was inviting friends and business associates. I realized that I had broken a long-standing rule about not inviting business contacts into my home. I told myself that I was doing it for a 'higher good.' But what *is* the higher good?"

It would be easy to allow every dinner party, bar mitzvah, wedding or political fundraiser to become an opportunity to add new names to your professional network. You must be vigilant or the skillful networking that has enabled your business to prosper will become the focus of *all* social occasions.

Perhaps it is unrealistic to think that business can be kept completely separate from the pleasure of your friendships. But if you cherish the value of your time after work, you need to exercise self-control to eliminate scenarios that expose the darker side of networking.

Scenario #1:
Here's My Card

Small business owners and fast-track professionals are apt to line even the pockets of their ski parkas with business cards. They know that every occasion offers the opportunity to promote business or self and to add to a business network.

Gene, the owner of a flower delivery service, admitted sheepishly, "I'm always looking for opportunities to pump up my business. Last week, my wife and I went to our first childbirth education class. Instead of getting to know the other people, I kept thinking: 'I've got to bring some business cards next time!'"

Your business card is *the* symbol of the visibility and the network of powerful contacts you want to cultivate. The pursuit of visibility in social situations contaminates old and new friendships and robs you of the opportunity to draw a clear line between work and play.

Friendships and social events need to be experienced in an arena that is separate from the staging of your self-promotion. It is essential to learn when to be invisible, when to pull in your net.

TECHNIQUE: Becoming Invisible

When Diana was planning her husband's birthday, she wondered, "Are all of my relationships utilitarian?"

It takes practice to refrain from thinking of every conversation as a job interview and every person as a potential client. You can avoid the discomfort of "expedient" friendships in several ways.

During the Work Week

- Join several professional organizations specifically for the purpose of building your networks. Examine possibilities with cool, professional criteria, asking, "Which group will provide the most connections for me?"
- Earmark several lunches, breakfasts or dinner meetings during the work week to follow up on new and old business contacts.

After Work

- Leave business cards at home when you attend social occasions. If you must make note of a business contact at a friend's wedding, use a cocktail napkin. Remember, you are there as a friend, not as a professional.
- Refuse to elaborate on your professional interests at special celebrations (see The Assertive Cocktail, page 145.) Change the subject and move on to more lighthearted topics.

Large celebrations can easily confuse business and friendly agendas.

Scenario #2:
The Tax Deductible Wedding

These are dreary affairs: the guest list is 50 percent clients, dress is conservative, the music is sedate and spouses respond to sexual innuendos with vague smiles.

Try not to compromise the important milestones in your life by inviting your closest friends to mingle with your business associates. You may gain tax advantages, but you'll lose an opportunity to celebrate and take time off for wild behavior.

I urge you to distinguish between business functions and joyous celebrations. Consider the following as business occasions, opportunities to make an impression or build your network:

- the company Christmas party
- an associate's wedding
- a retirement dinner
- a meeting of a professional association
- the office picnic
- a convention in Chicago.

Protect these events from your business agenda:

- your Golden Wedding anniversary
- your son's bar mitzvah
- your birthday
- a New Year's Eve party.

TECHNIQUE: "It's My Party and I'll Cry If I Want to . . ."

"Cry if I want to, cry if I want to. You would cry too, if it happened to you . . . ," sang Lesley Gore when I was a teenager.

Even with a broken heart, she had a good point: When you give a party, you should feel free to laugh, cry or overeat. If you mix friends and clients at parties, you may be unable to ignore the presence of your network. You will feel pressured by the need to maintain your professional image.

Afraid to appear out of control in front of your business associates, you'll deprive yourself of the opportunity to "cry if you want to," to learn new dance steps from your nephew or to lip-sync old Beatles songs.

One corporate vice-president explains the pressure of socializing with business associates: "I would *never* invite business contacts to a special dinner party. It does absolutely nothing for my 'power woman' image to be seen whipping up a soufflé in the kitchen!"

When you plan a special party, limit the guest list to friends.

With rare exceptions, your business associates do not care about you as a person. Their concern is with the business and services you can offer during working hours. Why include them at memorable occasions?

Draw a firm line between friendships cultivated for business and those for pleasure. You may lose the chance to gain a new client, but you gain the priceless time to enjoy friendships untouched by business concerns.

"DID YOU WORK THIS WEEKEND?"

My friend Peter describes a popular but defeating game that friends can play. "One of the reasons that I left Washington, D.C., was because of the emphasis on working overtime. No one ever asked, 'How was your weekend?' The question was 'Did you *work* this weekend?' Working evenings and weekends was something that friends bragged about. It was like a Purple Heart, a badge of courage."

Friends can help discourage each other from "working overtime" and invite each other to enjoy relaxing evenings and long weekends together.

Chapter 9

Play: Work in Disguise

A LONG WAY FROM THE OFFICE

My father, a doctor, can do a flawless impression of a Russian spy. It's been twenty years since our family talked him into accepting the role of Bibinski in a local production of *Silk Stockings*. I clearly recall my mother, a talented singer, coaching him on his lines and lyrics. But what I remember most is his big production number on opening night.

After singing and dancing his way through a number called "Hail Bibinski," he was hoisted high atop the shoulders of a dancer and paraded around the stage. I looked at his face, triumphant and half-terrified; he was a long way from his office.

My father's stage debut provided a lasting image of the pleasures of time after work. As he sang and mugged his way through the evening, he was satisfying needs that could not possibly be met in his medical practice.

This chapter explores the ways in which leisure can become an extension of work and suggests an alternative: that time after

140

work be directed at self-renewal, stimulation and the experience of rewards unlike those at work.

Start counting your 127 days off.

127 DAYS

If you calculate weekends, Sundays, holidays and at least two weeks of vacation, you will find that you have at least 127 days of leisure time each year. If you add the hours of evening after five, the time will increase substantially.

We all complain that we don't have enough time away from work, but how are you spending your precious leisure time?

To discover patterns in your free time, use one of the following two methods.

TECHNIQUE: Leisure Survey

Method 1

List activities you have enjoyed during the last three months. Did they take place during the week or weekend? Were they solo activities or done with friends or family? Was the goal relaxation, stimulation, adventure, community involvement, entertainment, personal growth, physical fitness?

Method 2

Dr. Gerald Forester, a University of Washington psychologist, suggests that you carry a packet of 3″ × 5″ cards for a week and make a note every time you change activities. Put each note on a different card.

This approach gives you an overview of your work and after-work activities. Make a special note of job-related activities: Do you extend your work skills and habits into your free time or do you compensate for intensive work by doing something very different?

AT YOUR LEISURE

As you recall and list your activities, you may begin to recognize a definite style to the way you spend your time after work. Do you recognize one of these patterns?

TGIF

The Thank God It's Friday style of thinking about leisure revolves around the habit of killing time until the weekend and then making the weekend truly memorable.

TGIF has spawned a series of related credos, like one overheard in the hall of an office building: "It's Tuesday; we're halfway there!" Restaurants in a chain called TGIF are packed every night after five.

A corporate vice-president, returning from a professional meeting, captured the "theory" of TGIF. Describing the national board meeting of a professional organization, she said, "They worked hard and they played hard."

The concept of playing hard has connotations of sexual and alcoholic excesses, yet for many participants in the TGIF style, playing hard simply means a deliberate change in activity: planning special getaways, buying tickets to a concert, inviting friends to dinner or looking forward to love in the afternoon. Dr. Tobin, for example, works sixty hours a week, but spends every weekend on his sailboat with his wife and kids.

Examine your leisure survey: Do you see a pattern of solid work commitments during the week and wall-to-wall activity on the weekends? This leisure style can be a positive choice in the sense that participants make definite plans to enjoy time after work. The drawback of the approach is that it tends to overcompensate for the stress and/or boredom of work and may lead to activities engaged in for the sole purpose of escape.

After a difficult week at work, the drive to escape may deprive you of opportunities to engage in stimulating and rewarding activities that can provide rich experiences that you don't get on the job.

Agitate-Vegetate

The motto of this after-work leisure style can be summed up in an ancient anonymous proverb: "How wonderful to do nothing and rest afterward."

The A-V leisure style has been adapted by millions of workers with high-stress jobs. As you examine your leisure survey, you may see a pattern of heated work activity followed by periods of minimal activity or passive entertainment.

A-Vers spend their evenings and weekends sleeping, lounging, watching television, being entertained. Julie, an industrial psychologist, explains, "I don't want to do a single thing on Saturday except sleep late, listen to relaxing music and talk to my husband and kids."

It is essential to use time after work for rest and recuperation from job pressures. If you recognize this leisure style, you know that you have learned to relax after work.

But don't assume that all other activities will add stress or further deplete your energy reserves. Keep your options open to consider other possibilities for intellectual or physical activity, for personal development or community involvement. You may be delighted and surprised to learn that sleeping and watching video movies are not the only ways to recover from the pressures of your job.

Camouflage

The lines at the movie were long and discouraging, and Lynn and Andy slipped into a nearby bowling alley. The first game was great fun, with both of them scoring in the high 80s.

During the second game, Andy got a series of strikes and started to take the game more seriously. Said Lynn, "He stopped laughing when he threw gutter balls and stepped up to the lane with a grim determination. Once Andy decided to 'get good at it,' I stopped enjoying the game. It had suddenly become work instead of play."

Leisure can easily become a camouflage for the attitudes and habits that we bring home from work. In Andy's case, the concern with attaining a high score replaced his enjoyment of an unlikely sport.

Although many of us enjoy competitive sports after work, we can draw a distinction between serious business and pleasure. It is important to play your best during the handball tournament, but the line is drawn at the point where you lose enjoyment of the game itself.

Review your leisure survey: Do you see patterns of activity where competition and performance are the focus of your free time? If ever the locker room motto "it's how you play the game" were appropriate, it's during the hours after work.

Concern with winning is only one of the ways that leisure becomes an extension of work. You may also find that your time after work is spent on activities that closely mirror your on-the-job responsibilities. You may be camouflaging work as play.

BUSMAN'S HOLIDAYS

Your time after work may be spent on busman's holidays with work activities thinly disguised as leisure. A busman's holiday is:

- A surgeon carving a Thanksgiving Day turkey
- Socrates hosting *The $64,000 Question*
- Michael Jackson singing in the shower
- Frankenstein working the graveyard shift
- An attorney watching *Perry Mason.*

Or you may find that the habits cultivated on the job contribute to unsatisfying leisure time.

At the end of a work day or week, you may discover that your bedside or deskside manner follows you home after work. Your occupational skills and habits of communicating, making decisions and managing people will not be appreciated by your friends and family. They will be the first to tell you:

A teenage daughter to her professor father: "I'm *not* one of your students, Dad."

The wife of a political lobbyist to her husband: "You can get off of your soapbox; we are only talking about a movie."

My husband, Jeremy, to me: "Let's not get so psychoanalytic about it. . . ."

Occupational habits can become hazardous to our health when we fail to turn them off after work. We also are at risk with friends and acquaintance who encourage us to continue working long hours and making "house calls."

OCCUPATIONAL HAZARDS

One hazard of your job may be that other people expect you to be wearing your professional hat at all times. Physicians, attorneys, psychologists, financial advisors, business owners and many others can be besieged at social gatherings with questions that call on their professional expertise.

Friends and acquaintances feel free to ask a doctor at halftime: "Syd, can you take a look at this mole behind my ear?" Or to ask the stockbroker passing the crudités: "Do you think I should buy AT&T now, or wait until things stabilize?"

Working professionals need to protect their private time from business inquiries. It is important to warmly but firmly refuse to talk about business or to render a service on the dance floor.

Giving free advice is not the issue; once you start talking about work, you are easily reminded of other problems, other cases you have left behind. You also forfeit the opportunity to allow friends and acquaintances to experience you in another, more relaxed role.

TECHNIQUE: The Assertive Cocktail

You're a lawyer and are enjoying a glass of wine and a conversation about the Super Bowl. A casual acquaintance marches up to you and asks: "My sister's husband moved in with his secretary.

Does that mean she will automatically get custody of the kids?"
You have three choices at that moment.

- You might give an *apologetic* response. Mumbling or shuf-
  fling your feet, you'd say: "Uh, I'm sorry, I don't handle
  family law cases. . . ."
- Maybe you'll answer with an *aggressive* response. In a
  loud and tight voice you might ask: "What do you think
  this is, night court?"
- Your best response would be to change the subject in an
  assertive, friendly manner. Smile and say: "That's a good
  question, but I'm taking the night off."

Practice saying each of these responses in three ways: first,
apologetically, then *aggressively*, then *assertively*.

1. "Sorry, but I left my calculator (stethoscope, slide rule,
   briefcase) in the office."
2. "That's an interesting problem, but I was hoping to stay
   out of court (the office, the hospital) this weekend."
3. "You sound concerned. I can talk to you about it on
   Monday (tomorrow). Why don't you call me at the office?"
4. "I wish you had asked me that before I had my third
   glass of champagne. I'll have to take two aspirin and call
   you in the morning!"

When you refuse to mix business and pleasure, your friends
and acquaintances lose an opportunity for free advice but gain a
chance to engage you in topics unrelated to your work interest.

Protecting your leisure time is part of the process of learning
to use time after work to counterbalance the skills, habits and
satisfactions you experience on the job.

SCHOOL FOR PLAY

Education for leisure was the focus of a classical Greek education. Aristotle suggested that *leisure*, rather than work, provided the purest definition of the self.

In our society, we have little education for leisure but do put considerable emphasis on a "balanced" life. In the balance of work and leisure, the key is using leisure time to satisfy needs that your job does not provide.

Take a moment to think about your balancing of needs at work and after work. Consider each of these areas of potential satisfaction in your life (adapted from Jan Gault's *Free Time*). Which of your needs are satisfied at work? After work?

- Physical Activity
- Entertainment
- Sensory Stimulation
- Personal Growth
- Social Responsibility
- Creative Expression
- Relaxation
- Spirituality
- Sense of Accomplishment
- Community Involvement
- Solitude
- Intellectual Challenge
- Spirit of Adventure
- Close Contact with People
- Recognition
- Opportunity to Develop Friendships

If your job lacks opportunities in an area of potential satisfaction, have you compensated for this in your time after work? As you think about the counterbalances in your life, consider several examples.

Accomplishment/Creativity

I'm not suggesting that your time after work be devoted to activity diametrically opposed to work. In fact, many business and professional people enjoy much satisfaction by applying their job skills in radically different settings.

Business Volunteers for the Arts is a perfect example of this approach to balance. In New York, Los Angeles, Seattle, San Francisco, Houston and Philadelphia, business executives volunteer weekly to work with nonprofit arts groups. Bankers, accountants and consultants of every description are paired with the artists and the boards of directors from opera and ballet companies, avant-garde theater groups or chamber ensembles.

The banker who applies his budget skills to become involved in a creative collaboration with a struggling theater group has satisfied needs that go beyond his corporate application of financial skill.

Close Contact/Solitude

The frequency and intensity of your contacts with people at work will influence the balance of social time after work.

Dennis spends most of the day alone, feeding numbers into the payroll computer of a large company. He makes a point of scheduling several evenings a week with friends for dinner or a drink.

Jean is a psychologist whose days are spent in intense dialogue with her patients. "Everything has *meaning* when you do therapy; nothing is taken for granted. When I come home, I enjoy time alone or lighthearted conversations with my family or friends."

Self-Promotion/Community Involvement

Most professionals and small-business owners spend their work week in relentless promotion (see The Darker Side of Networking, page 135). For them, time after work can be balanced by strong community participation.

Dana is the owner of an elegant women's clothing store. After work, she is deeply involved in the consumer rights movement, attending meetings, planning speakers, raising funds. She feels comfortable in the balance of promoting her business and contributing to the positive future of her community.

A DIFFERENT BALANCE

As you examine the balance of work and leisure in your life, you may see possibilities for change but feel limited by a lack of ideas, projects or activities to shift the balance. Consult a leisure reference guide like *The Leisure Alternatives Catalogue* to help stimulate possibilities of participation in a broad spectrum of after-work activities. Include sports, entertainment, arts, crafts-manship, educational enrichment, collecting, games, political organizing, environmental activism and contributions to your community in your search.

You may have grand ideas and strong intentions, but you find yourself making, and cancelling plans to enrich your time after work. It may be helpful to set up a series of obstacles to help you keep your commitments to special leisure time.

TECHNIQUE: Following Through

- Buy season tickets to sports events, theater shows and concerts, and write the dates on your calendar. Having made the arrangements, you will be less likely to cancel.
- Plan leisure activities with friends. It is easier to cancel plans for yourself than to break up a doubles tennis match.
- When you volunteer, sign up for specific times and dates.
- When you book ski trips and cabins on the ocean, pay in advance. Preregister for classes and lecture series. Your financial investment may prevent you from cancelling.
- Announce your intentions to other people. Having talked about your trip to the Caribbean for weeks, you don't want to explain to thirty-five people why you don't have a tan.

Whether you spend your time after work whale watching, stargazing, learning French or raising funds for Friends of the Symphony, you have worked hard to earn your free time. Plan to make it a time of meaning and delight.

Part
FOUR

THE
WORKING
FAMILY

Chapter 10

Unwinding:
For Parents
And Kids

As a parent, you could measure the end of the day in units of transitions per minute. You must adjust to leaving your workplace, to the presence of a spouse and to the needs of your children.

Dan, a management consultant, describes the situation: "First, I pick up Cyndy at her office, then we drive to the day-care center to collect our daughter. As we drive home, we are like three people coming home from work, all of us wanting to process our day at the same time."

While you are at work, your children are experiencing a series of stresses and triumphs that are parallel to your own. When you greet your children, the success of your evening will depend, in part, on how each of you has dealt with the day's problems.

This chapter underlines the importance of transition techniques for working parents, reviews the pressures of a child's "day at school" and suggests quick and efficient techniques for parents who have little time to unwind.

Let's begin with the baby-sitter's report and with the stresses lurking in the classroom and on the playground.

WHAT THE BABY-SITTER SAW

As the parent of an infant or preschool child, you will be greeted by a baby-sitter or a day-care worker at the end of the day. At the same time as you are reviewing your day, the baby-sitter is providing you with the highlights of your child's day.

Important areas of review include how the young child ate and slept, which toys he or she enjoyed, and how he or she responded to the sitter, teacher and other children.

Janet, a banker, describes picking up her seven-week-old baby at an infant development center. "At the end of the day, they'd tell us about her mood, her responsiveness and her eye movements. But my husband and I were so exhausted, all I remember about those first six months of being back at work is coming home and lying down on the couch. My main topic of conversation with Ken was 'Are we more tired than we are hungry?'"

School-age children will tell you very directly about their day and may expect your full attention.

HOW CHILDREN COME HOME FROM SCHOOL

"When I pick up my daughter," one father reported, "I am suddenly thrust into the world of children."

Within that world, each of the problems outlined in the first chapter may also concern your school-age child. Children have their own version of a fast pace, unfinished symphonies and encounters with difficult people. They come home with unexpressed feelings about these people and pressures—feelings that may greet you and demand to be heard as you walk through the front door.

Here is a child-size inventory of the stresses of the day.

The Fast Lane

During a typical school day, younger children cover basic subject matter in swift, hourly chunks. By lunchtime, your son may have tackled problems in long division, completed a watercolor drawing, taken a spelling test and learned that George Washington had false teeth.

In high school, your daughter is solving for x one hour and conjugating a verb in French an hour later. She steps off the volleyball court and walks into her economics class. Tonight, she may be able to explain supply-side economics.

After the age of seven or eight, most school-age children rapidly shift gears to a series of after-school activities as diverse as cub scouts, Junior Achievement, music lessons, drama club or just hanging out with friends. A therapist and the mother of a nine-year-old commented: "Jonathan's schedule is beginning to look like mine!"

And the parents of teenagers will soon be pleading to be kept informed about the social calendars of their children. "We have reached the 'Where are you going?' stage," lamented one parent.

This rapid pace leaves many young people tired at the end of the day, and the numerous activities create many opportunities to carry home unfinished business.

Unfinished Symphonies

The youthful version of unfinished business usually takes the form of homework: a math test, a science project or three chapters of *The Scarlet Letter* to be read by tomorrow.

Other unfinished business involves a series of logistical problems that will require your attention. These can include a note for the school field trip, clay for an art project, your signature on a driver's permit form or cookies for a school open house.

Social agendas are another source of concern. There are parties to be planned, friends invited to spend the night, dates accepted and rejected and phone calls to return.

Along with their social calendar, kids of all ages come home with strong feelings about the people in their day.

Uninvited Guests

Often your children will literally bring a friend home. On other occasions—much to your dismay—your first hour at home will be spent listening to a blow-by-blow description of your son's teacher.

Depending on the age of your kids, the following uninvited guests may become regulars at your dinner table.

- *The kids on the bus*
  "Susan said I was fat. I'm not fat, am I?"

- *Fair-weather friends*
  "I don't trust her anymore. She told Alice everything I said."

- *Young Love*
  "I don't trust her anymore. She told *Greg* everything I said."

Unexpressed Feelings

Your child's feelings about important people and unfinished business may be very strong, but they may be camouflaged and unspoken. They may be communicated to you in code.

Diana, an accountant, is familiar with veiled messages. "I can always tell when my teenage son is upset. He'll pick a fight and go back one hundred years. He will say, 'Remember that time you wouldn't let me go to the Rolling Stones concert?' If we continue talking, and I can keep my temper, I will usually find out that something at school or a conflict with a friend is the real source of the problem."

But keeping your temper while your children unwind from school can be a Herculean task.

UNWINDING WITH YOU AND WITHOUT YOU

School-age kids have opportunities to unwind before they see you. Your children may take the bus, walk or ride bikes home from school. Often accompanied by their friends, they trade gossip and secrets; they swap homework and assurances. They debrief the day among friends.

Many kids play physical games after school: bicycling, soccer,

Frisbee and football. Kids of all ages watch TV and create snacks of every possible description.

Younger children seem to want company after school and teenagers seem to cherish the time alone. Sharon, thirteen, describes her homecoming rituals. "When I am walking home, I feel tired. I walk in the door and fix myself a cup of tea. I turn on the TV and stare at it; I'm not really watching it, but I'm trying not to think about my day."

For most kids, the ritual of unwinding after school is not complete until you come home or pick them up at school or the baby-sitter's.

Nancy, an interior designer, asked her son Daniel, twelve and her daughter Miriam, nine: "What is the first thing you want when I walk through the front door?"

"I want attention," said Miriam. "I want you to hug me and let me tell you about school."

"Not me," said Daniel. "I want to know what's for dinner."

These needs are typical of the situations that face you when you walk through the front door after work. Your children want your warm greetings and an opportunity to gain your ear. They may also make immediate demands about domestic responsibilities—like laundry and dinner.

Most parents look forward to seeing their children at the end of the day. Greg, a management consultant, describes his daughter as "*the* reason to work hard at making the transition after work." Parents enjoy the process of "show and tell." The problem is that the "show" often begins the moment they walk through the door—before they have had time to unwind from the pressures of work.

If you hope to respond warmly to the immediate needs of your family, it is absolutely essential to have given yourself a chance to unwind before coming home. But time is a precious commodity to working parents.

You'll need quick and efficient techniques to accomplish the transition from harried professional to loving parent.

UNWINDING AT 100 MILES PER HOUR

A working mother, who was attending one of my workshops about coming home, became exasperated and said: "These techniques for transition are straight from Fantasyland. I don't have *time* to unwind before I see my kids!"

She was right about the time shortage. Parents need to unwind and adjust to coming home more quickly than other working people. But she was mistaken to think that she could head straight for home.

Every working person needs to incorporate rituals that acknowledge the end of the day and the beginning of an evening at home. Parents who skip this step put their families at risk.

Diana, a single parent, isn't willing to take the risk. "I need time to walk away from my work situation. Sometimes I'll pay the sitter an extra three dollars so I can go to the gym. The damage I do in the first five minutes can ruin the evening with my son. If I exercise, I feel that when I come home, I'm there to stay."

Parents—and especially single parents—don't have time after work for a two-hour bubble bath à la Nancy Reagan. But every parent should allot at least a small amount of time in which to disengage from the pressures of work.

Limited time means that as a parent, you will have to be creative and nimble in accomplishing your transitional rituals; it doesn't mean that you skip them. You may need to combine techniques of unwinding with some of the responsibilities of family life.

There is no question that you will be moving at a speed of 100 miles per hour. Why not practice some of the techniques while grocery shopping or picking up your daughter from softball practice?

Let's reexamine the five problems of homecoming and consider the most time-efficient techniques to reduce the problems.

Problem: Slowing Down

In Chapter 1, I suggested that you might slow down by saving the easiest tasks of the day for last. I also suggested a five-minute trip to Tahiti (see page 26). If you don't feel comfortable sitting still for five minutes or if you have trouble visualizing, try an alternative vacation.

TECHNIQUE: Four Fast Vacations

As you drive or ride the bus or train home, you can use a series of sounds to transport yourself to a more restful location. Mike Kron, an acoustician at New York-based Syntonic Research, describes a number of albums and cassettes called Environments that can be purchased at local record stores.

Choose among four fast vacations:

- *Sailboat*
  Kron calls this tape "the most effective for sitting on the freeway." The sounds include the wind whipping against the sails, the waves lapping up against the boat. One listener reported that in traffic jam "the car became a sailboat."

- *Ocean*
  An instant walk on the beach. The rhythmic sound of the waves breaking on shore can help eliminate the noise of cars, diesel buses, subway trains.

- *An English Meadow*
  This tape was prepared in Sussex, England, and invites you into a meadow at dawn, complete with melodious birds and rustling leaves.

- *Thunderstorm*
  Recorded atop a Manhattan apartment, this tape lets you enjoy the cozy, relaxed feeling of being indoors during a thunderstorm. It is punctuated by the sound of rain hitting the pavement and of distant thunder.

Tape addicts have reported that they use the tapes on headsets and in cars on their way home. Others listen when they get home. One happy listener reported, "These tapes have replaced my martini."

But you may be thinking, "I can't listen to the tapes. I have to pick up my kids on my way home."

TECHNIQUE: **Four Fast Family Vacations**

You can plan to include other family members on your brief vacations. If you play the tapes in the car, explain to your kids that the sounds help you to relax, to feel good.

Don't be surprised if your children become absorbed in the sounds. Mike Kron explains, "The strongest application of the environmental tapes has been to help students of all ages study. They are a means of stimulating imagination that has been used by teachers all over the country."

Even if the family doesn't listen in silence, the background can have a soothing effect on the conversation and on you. "In some cases," reports Kron, "the tapes can become associated with a particular activity. Think of the possibilities: Your family might think of the ride home as a walk through a meadow or a jaunt on a sailboat."

Even on a sailboat, you may have been thinking about the work problems that pursue you.

Problem: Postponing Unfinished Business

With so little time to unwind, you may want to delegate tasks to the resources of your unconscious mind (see page 24). The application of thought stopping (see page 25) will also help postpone thoughts about your unfinished business.

For another speedy means of closure, practice a technique perfected by a working parent.

TECHNIQUE: **"Good-bye, Office"**

Diana, a warm and witty therapist, describes her special technique of postponing office business. "I decided to get more formal about saying good-bye at the end of the day. I used to casually say to my secretary and associates, 'So long, see you tomorrow.' Now I make a point of finding each one and saying good-bye more formally. I walk outside of my office, close the door and say, '*good-bye, office*.'"

She continues, "Just as important, when I see my son, I make a special effort to give him more than a casual greeting. I make a big point of saying hello with a hug and a kiss. I put into words how glad I am to see him."

Practice mentally closing the doors to your office and saying "Good-bye, office" on your way home to your family. This technique takes less than a minute and provides definite recognition of the end of the day.

Problem: Feelings About Difficult People

As you end the day, make time for a brief emotional conference with yourself. This can be accomplished by rolling the credits (see page 28) and connecting with your feelings about the important people in your day.

Strong feelings about work often have no place to go. How about putting them in a plain brown wrapper?

TECHNIQUE: The Boss's Brown Paper Bag

Sharon, a market researcher, likes to keep a brown paper bag on the front seat of her car. Her previous boss suggested this technique.

"He said that before coming to work, he would place the bag over his mouth and talk about each of his concerns. He'd try to talk about his wife and kids and then leave his feelings *in the bag* so that he could concentrate on work."

After work, you can collect all of your feelings about difficult people in the same paper bag and leave it on the front seat of the car. This silly and symbolic act may help you to regain your sense of humor.

Problem: Loss of Humor

Facing your family without a sense of humor can be a dangerous mission. Yet the day may have left you drained, without a giggle in sight. The fastest technique for finding humor can involve a game with one of your children.

TECHNIQUE: The Funniest Thing

Joel Goodman, a father and editor of the journal *Laughing Matters*, describes a game that a parent and child can play. It can recharge a sense of humor.

The rules are simple. Each working day, both parent and child share a ritual dialogue together. Each one takes a turn, telling or asking: "What is the funniest or nuttiest thing that happened to you today?"

As you leave work, review your day for comic material. Using hints in Chapter 2, select one event and transform it into a funny story.

Knowing that your child expects to hear a comic tale can help revive your battered sense of humor. Exchanging funny stories is a way of easing the transition and developing the habit of good humor in your family.

Problem: Self-Absorption

Everyone who spends the day concentrating on work will be focused on his or her own thought at the end of the day. Happily, the problem of self-absorption can be addressed by eavesdropping (see page 70) or staring (see page 71) during errands on your way home.

Even pulp newspapers and magazines can help reduce your self-absorption; it may be better to wonder about Paul McCartney's latest drug arrest than to remain preoccupied with your boss's nasty habits.

After you have rerouted your thoughts by focusing on strangers, you are ready to use the technique of glimpsing (see page 71) to create a mental picture of family members waiting for you at home.

Some parents prefer to preview their evenings at home with a phone call.

TECHNIQUE: Previewing

Many working parents ask their children to call them at work when they got home. Whether your child is home alone or with a baby-sitter, a telephone preview can help prevent you from being overwhelmed by a barrage of stories and demands when you walk through the door.

Listening to your child talk briefly about the day gives you a preview of emotional needs and logistical demands. You can learn, for example, that your son was disappointed because he didn't get selected for the school play or that your daughter needs special glue for her science project.

Sometimes a parent can miss crucial information in a previewing phone call. One mother reported a phone call in which her son had "some good news and some bad news." "Of course, I told him, 'Tell me the good news first.' We talked for three minutes about how pleased he was about his score on a math test. Then I said, 'What's the bad news?' 'The bad news is about Jimmy,' he said quickly. 'Two kids are beating him up outside!'"

MAKING YOUR ENTRANCE

If you don't take the time to unwind after work, you may lose the opportunity to enjoy the evening with your children. Coming home exhausted and preoccupied with the problems of your day, you may react with anger or guilt to the immediate demands of family life.

In the next chapter, we'll consider some memorable entrances and several ways to create a more enjoyable transition when you walk through the front door.

Chapter 11

"Your Parents Are Home"

When you give yourself a brief time to confront the five problems that accompany the end of your workday, you can arrive at home with some semblance of sanity and good cheer.

If you arrive with a briefcase full of undigested feelings, you may spend the rest of the evening undoing the effects of your first appearance. Confronted with the immediate emotional and logistical demands of your family, you may be unable to respond with love and affection. Instead, you could remind your children of two characters from the pages of their storybooks.

The Queen of Hearts

Alice had been in Wonderland for only a short time when she learned that the Queen of Hearts was something less than an enlightened despot.

The Queen had absolutely no tolerance for frustration or conflict. At the first sign of a problem, she would issue her famous brittle command: "Off with his head!" Weary with the demands of reigning her kingdom, she felt justified in her self-indulgent commands and capricious punishments.

For many exhausted parents, particularly those who are greeted at the door by fighting siblings, the threshold of the door can quickly become a scaffold.

Norma, a designer, confesses to past moments of self-indulgence: "If I had a hard day, I'd either walk through the door and blow up or run upstairs and take a shower, whichever I got to *first!*" In the past couple of years, I have learned to discipline myself, to go through my kids' rituals first, to meet their needs first, and *then* to go upstairs and change my clothes and wash my face."

Exercising self-control when you walk through the front door takes a strong, concerted effort. Your kids may want the most attention from you at the moment when you have the least to give.

Some days you will feel like you are about to metamorphose into the Queen of Hearts. Before you start to order beheadings—or the parental equivalent of grounding—why not hold court for a few minutes?

TECHNIQUE: Holding Court

Holding court when you come home from work means that for the first ten or fifteen minutes you concentrate all of your attention on your children and then excuse yourself for some royal recuperation.

Monica, a real estate broker, describes the technique: "Sandra has been home for a couple of hours alone by the time I get home. She sees me and she wants to spell out everything! She wants to talk about homework, and her girlfriends and boyfriend and plans for the weekend. I listen to her for a couple of minutes, and *then* I say hello to George and take off my coat!"

Holding court can protect your homecoming from catastrophe. For a brief period of time, focus on the immediate needs of your children. Then you can excuse yourself, without guilt, for a moment of silence.

But maybe you make your entrance already feeling guilty.

Hansel and Gretel's Father

Hansel and Gretel's father was feeling guilty, and who could blame him? He worked as a woodcutter, barely eking out a living, and on the day in question, he allowed his new wife to talk him into abandoning his children in the forest.

The children's stepmother outlined the plan: "Tomorrow we will take the children to the heart of the forest, give them each a piece of bread; then we will go back to our work and they will never be able to find their way back home." This guilty father did not enjoy a single joyous moment until Hansel and Gretel, through a series of storybook coincidences, returned home.

Hansel and Gretel's father was a parent who felt overcome by remorse and with good reason. Yet so many parents sour their own homecoming with crippling feelings of guilt that are *not* based in reality.

Working mothers, in particular, can come home feeling and acting as if they have abandoned their children in the forest. Guilt feelings keep these parents from taking time to practice techniques for unwinding, and propel them into spending every minute of the evening with their child.

Tanya, a marketing specialist, explains: "When I come home, I want to spend a little time alone. But I feel guilty—I feel I owe my daughter the time. I think: If I were a better parent, I'd be more available to her at the end of the day."

Many working parents experience uncomfortable feelings about not being a "good enough parent." Other parents feel guilty because their thoughts about their children are not totally positive, or because they resent how their children infringe on their leisure time or time together as partners.

Guilt feelings are based on an equation between what is ideal behavior and what is actual behavior. If the gap between your ideal expectations and your everyday behavior is too great, you can be overwhelmed by guilt.

Guilt is a sad substitute for the delight and frustrations of family life; it is a distracting emotion. You can reduce the distraction by exploring the source of your ideal expectations and putting them into words.

TECHNIQUE: Consider the Source

Every family has a set of unwritten ideals about family life. Think back to your own family and attempt to list some of the attitudes and expectations about being a family that were conveyed to you by your own parents and extended family. Try to recall your own ideals as you grew toward parenthood.

You can stimulate your memory by filling in the blanks in the following sentences. Write in the first thing that comes to mind.

1. My father felt that when a baby was born a man should _____.

   My mother thought a woman should _____

   _____.

2. My parents always felt that children should be ____

   _____ but not _____

   _____.

3. In my family, my mother always

   1._____

   2._____

4. In my family, my father always

   1._____.

   2._____.

5. My parents felt that their relationship (a) came before
   the kids; (b) was secondary to us. I knew this because

   _____.

   _____.

6. When I was growing up, I always thought that
   _____ was a good parent because _____.
   (name)

7. When I was growing up, I had a list of things I would
   NEVER do if I became a parent. My list included:

   _____

   _____

8. I also had a list of things I would ALWAYS do if I
   became a parent. My list included:

   _____

   _____.

Now go through the list and answer the questions from your present point of view. Note the differences and discuss them with your spouse or a close friend.

Your past is not the only source of the ideals and expectations that you use for inducing guilt. Consider any of your peers that you think are ideal parents or any movies, TV shows or books that excited you about the possibilities of parenting.

Take an honest look at the real and legendary parental ideals you are carrying as you make your entrance after work. These may be keeping you from enjoying your strengths and limitations as a parent. Instead of coming home like a guilty character, learn to recognize the source of your unrealisitic expectations and to treat your best attempts with humor and generosity.

Brad, a single parent and physician, captures the essence of this self-acceptance as a parent. "Sometimes I think I ought to be giving my daughter more time. But, damn it, I'm tired and sometimes I give her some things she can play with on her own. I mean, I can only play Chutes and Ladders so many times!"

Another father who delights in seeing his daughter warmly acknowledges the loss of his own leisure time and his time alone with his wife. He laughs and warns, "Don't ever let *anyone* tell you that having kids won't change your relationship!"

Families can develop a repertoire of good habits, supported by the idea of realistic expectations for both parents and children. Such habits will prevent guilty and self-indulgent characters from making an entrance.

GOOD HABITS START EARLY

I saw a charming commercial directed to parents. The ad shows a grade school class on a field trip. The teacher does a quick head count and discovers that one of the children is missing. A frantic search uncovers her whereabouts; she is in the bathroom brushing her teeth. The commentary: "Good habits start early."

The tone of your family life and your children's habits are guided by the behavior you model and the suggestions and expectations you communicate from their earliest years.

Consider seven good habits that can add grace and joy to your family's transition after work and school.

Good Habit #1:
Encourage Activities
That Help Family Members to Unwind

This habit can begin by your example. Let your children know at an early age that you are involved in various activities that help you unwind after work. Even a four-year-old can understand these explanations:

> "Come talk to me while I jump (on the trampoline) or ride the bike. I am really tired today. I think riding will help me wake up."

> "I'm going to run upstairs and change my clothes. I love to put on a sweatshirt—like the one you have—when I get home."

The idea of unwinding might be inaugurated by a simple conversation.

PARENT: Do you ever feel tired after school?
CHILD: Sometimes.
PARENT: What do you do when you feel tired?
CHILD: I don't know, maybe take a nap or watch TV.
PARENT: Sometimes I feel tired when I get home, too. Taking a run really gives me energy. When I feel refreshed, we can have more fun together after dinner.

Showing that you need to unwind is an ideal way to introduce the idea of transition to your family. You can also encourage your kids to structure their time after school to meet some of their own needs. Here are some possibilities:

- *Show an interest in activities besides school and schoolwork.*
  Don't just ask, "What did you do in school?" You can also ask, "What did you do *after* school?"

- *Don't insist that homework be done before dinner.*
  Suggest that the work needs to be done by 8 o'clock and let your child decide whether he or she wants to get it out of the way or to hang out and do it after dinner.

- *Encourage activities that help kids unwind.*
  Let them spend time on the phone to friends (within limits) or time visiting friends. Stock nutritious snacks, like fruit, vegetable sticks, wholesome cookies. '

- *Encourage them to exercise after school through bike rides with friends, school sports, walks with you.*
  Remember that the "fight or flight" impulse is alive in children, too; kids have accumulated tensions throughout the day.

- *Expose them to the possibilities of after-school interests (besides TV) that will help them relax.*
  Browse with your child in a hobby store and see if anything catches his or her eye. Encourage your son or daughter to collect anything of interest, including stamps, bottles, coins, rock star autographs.

  Visit bookstores and let each child buy the book of his or or her choice. Let each choose a magazine; sign them up for a subscription and let them watch for it in the mail.

  Take your kids to the ballet, symphony, popular concerts (until they reach the age when they won't be seen with you) and jazz performances. Allow for the possibility of dance or music lessons.

  Buy them an inexpensive stereo or tape deck and let them listen to their choice of music. You might also invest in earphones.

Good Habit #2:
Encourage Your Family to
Put Their Feelings into Words

The good habit of talking about feelings begins with your example. Anna, a corporate attorney, believes that her own openness encourages her children to talk about school.

"I try not to just pry. So I try to say something about my day, too. I can be honest; I can admit I had a crummy day. When I open up to my son, he seems to open up to me, too. He'll tell me about something that is bothering him, and I'll commiserate and say: 'It sounds like a bad day for both of us; the stars must have been in the wrong place!'"

It is important to set limits on how much you disclose to your children. Editing is important in these conversations. Anna can't expect her son to understand the labyrinth of corporate politics, but she can identify some basic feelings about her day. Her son will understand his mother's essential, unspoken message: "I am willing to talk."

If your son or daughter doesn't volunteer information, you can *try* to ask questions. This is a delicate maneuver because you don't want to nag or pry. Be prepared to ask several questions and then to retreat and respect your child's privacy.

The best questions are those that are "essay" questions followed by *paraphrasing*, rather than *advice*.

TECHNIQUE: Closed Questions, Multiply Choices, Essays

School-age children can easily recognize the difference between a closed question, an essay and a multiple choice. Closed questions and multiple choices take only a second to answer and don't allow for an expansive response. An essay question allows for a more detailed, richer answer.

Your questions about your child's day need to be gentle, interested probes; they are not a test. But be careful or the questioning process may remind your kids of a pop quiz.

Closed Question

PARENT: (noticing that son is particularly quiet) Did you have a bad day today?

SON: No.

End of conversation. If your goal is to allow for a discussion of feelings, try not to ask a question that can be answered by a yes or no. You'd want a yes/no answer if you asked whether the meat loaf was in the oven.

Multiple Choice

PARENT: You seem quiet. Are you tired, are you upset with David or did that math test wipe you out?

DAUGHTER: I am just tired.

End of conversation. Try not to ask multiple-choice questions. Kids will choose one of the choices and the potential for shared feelings may be lost.

Essay Question

PARENT: You seem quiet. Something about school wasn't the greatest?

DAUGHTER: You can say that again. Debbie decided to work with someone else on our science project.

Essay questions give your son or your daughter a chance to describe a difficult or exciting situation. This initial description will also give you the opportunity to look for feelings that you can paraphrase.

Review the art of paraphrasing in Chapter 6. After your child has answered an essay question, you'll be able to paraphrase the feelings and situation so that the conversation can continue.

DAUGHTER: You can say that again. Debbie decided to work with someone else on our science project.

PARENT: You were really counting on her, and she let you down.

DAUGHTER: I thought she was my friend. I don't see how she could change her mind like that. . . .

This is a conversation that has a future. Learn to ask open-ended questions that can be followed by a restatement of the strong feeling your child expresses.

You will also learn to be comfortable with silence. Sometimes even the most eloquent essay questions fail to elicit a response.

When this happens, smile warmly and say, "I can see that you don't feel like talking right now. Let me know if you change your mind."

Good Habit #3:
Encourage Family Members to Understand Each Other's Point of View

Families adjust more easily to changes and transitions when they can empathize or see the world through someone else's eyes.

Empathy is grounded in the capacity to picture another person's situation. The art of paraphrasing is an empathic skill, but younger children cannot be expected to paraphrase *your* feelings.

Still, the capacity to understand others is a habit that can begin early with family field trips and games.

TECHNIQUE: Field Trips

There is a marvelous scene in the movie *Kramer vs. Kramer,* where the advertising executive, played by Dustin Hoffman, takes his son up to his high-rise office. His son plays at his desk and takes in his father's world.

You can bring your children of all ages on a field trip to your office. Show them your desk, some of your work in progress. Have them meet your secretary or co-workers.

If you don't feel comfortable introducing your family into your professional setting, bring the kids in on Saturday. The ability to picture you at work is a first step in the development of empathy.

Carla is a sales representative whose family has developed a dinner hour game to learn to take each other's perspective.

TECHNIQUE: Trading Places

In this game, family members sit in each other's usual place. Next, they take on the role of the person who usually sits in the chair.

Carla explains, "Tim sits in my chair and imitates me talking about my day. I sit in his chair; I imitate his table manners and talk about his teachers. The game leads to lots of laughter and denial: 'I don't do that, do I?'"

Carla's family is happily involved in the process of developing the habit of empathy. Observing and imitating other family members can be a first step in learning to understand the world from their perspective.

Good Habit #4:
Encourage Each Person to Contribute to Family Life

My sister Cora describes a wonderful dinner party hosted by our niece and nephew, Hilary, age eight, and Adam, ten. The menu: falafel, salad, sweet rolls, macaroni and a castle cake covered with gumdrops. Their mother provided baked chicken.

"No wine was served because the special beverage was a drink concocted from milk, orange sherbet and 7-Up. Adam kept asking me, 'Can I get you a refill?' The best part of the dinner was that the kids were so proud of themselves."

You can encourage the habit of making a contribution when your kids come home from school. Too many homecomings are marred by the crush to take care of logistics, like making dinner or doing the wash.

Kids feel proud of their involvement at home, and when you take care of domestic chores together, you can allow for more creative and playful time.

Lucia, a college administrator, reported, "When my kids were two and three years old, they started to help to get dinner ready. They would set the table, cut up the fruit and spill the juice all over the floor. . . . But they felt important, involved. I heard them tell their friends that they helped at home. And we had more time together for talks and for stories."

The key to developing the habit of contributing is to have reasonable expectations and to lower your own standards. The kids may add too much soap to the wash or leave spots on the glasses; they may put the fork on the wrong side of the plate.

Follow some guidelines for encouraging their contributions.

- *Don't expect them to do things the way you would.*

If they tear up the lettuce for a salad, don't complain if you get a piece the size of a palm leaf.

- *Choose tasks that are reasonable for each age.*
  A four-year-old can wash tomatoes for a salad. A ten-year-old can turn on the dishwasher.

- *Don't overload them so that they don't have time to unwind from school.*

- *Always praise them for their contribution.*
  Help them understand that cooperation can lead to more relaxed time with you.

Don't expect too much. They are, after all, just kids. Adam, the orange-drink host, reminded his mother of this fact when she asked him to make the quiche recipe he had learned at school. He refused, saying, "I want to play on the playground, for God sakes!"

Good Habit #5:
Encourage a Sense of Timing

Time management is an adult-size concept, the subject of thousands of words in print and a centerpiece of corporate training. But the ability to utilize a sense of timing doesn't begin on a first job. It is a habit that can be developed early.

If your children can develop some sense of timing, you can ease the transition between work and home. You'll be able to cut down on the number of urgent logistical requests that eat up your evenings and reduce the family's leisure time on the weekends.

You can encourage a sense of timing in these ways:

- *Teach your kids to anticipate their needs for money and errands whenever possible.*
  You can expect them to keep an eye on library book due dates or on a lunch ticket with two more punches. Ask them to list anticipated needs on a family "to do" list.

- *Discourage the concept of "this will only take a minute."*

Help teach your kids to estimate how long it takes to do a task, errand or playful pastime.

Explain, for example, that they can't shop for shoes, get help on a science project and go to a matinee on Saturday from 1 o'clock to 3 o'clock. Estimate time out loud for them. "Let's see, the shoes will probably take thirty minutes and the movie is two hours long. . . ."

- *Encourage them to think about what is most important.*
  If you can't accomplish everything on Saturday, ask: "What is the most important?" Let them answer, "The shoes, I guess. I need them on Monday. Maybe we could work on my project tomorrow."

- *You can teach them about scheduling with a family calendar posted in the kitchen.*
  Hold regular family conferences to juggle schedules.

- *Help them learn to respect your time, too.*
  You are available to them, but you may need advance notice. One father and mother require at least twenty-four hours warning to attend a PTA meeting.

Kids need to know that you are responsive to their needs but that you also need time to take care of your own needs. In particular, you need time to spend alone and with your partner or friends.

Good Habit #6:
Encourage the Recognition of Private Time

It was probably inevitable: a set of greeting cards for working parents. One card shows a suited woman coming home with the message, "Every working mother is entitled to some time alone." Open the card and you see her surrounded by three kids, a dog and a cat, each demanding her immediate attention. The card reads: *"Time's up!"*

Even when your children are young, you can begin to show them that time alone is an important part of family life. Many a homecoming is ruined by the prospect of partners who have no time alone, or time together.

Many parents feel guilty about wanting to be alone with their spouse. It is important to remember that a strong marriage, nurtured by rich communication and sexual expression, is the foundation of a happy family.

You can express the value of private time in a number of ways:

- *Respect your children's need for private time.*
  This need will be strongest beginning with the preteen years. One father explains, "When I come home I make a point of hugging my daughter and saying hello, but I leave her alone in her room until she is ready to talk to me."

- *Make a date with each child for some private one-to-one time.*
  Taking your daughter to lunch or to a movie can help her to understand the private time you spend with your friends and partner.

- *Communicate the strong value of private time.*
  If you trade off private time with your partner, let your children know that Mom's evening with her friends is special and important.

- *Try to introduce your desire for time alone with affection.*
  It is important that your children grow up with the understanding that your time spent alone is not a punishment for them, it is a special and essential time for you.

- *Learn to feel comfortable closing your doors after 9:00 o'clock and allowing for sweet time with your partner.*
  Explain warmly, "Mom and Dad need time to talk and to feel close to each other."

Good Habit # 7:
Encourage Family Members to Talk About Topics Besides Work and School

Among my dearest memories of growing up are the discussions that enlivened my family's dinner table. This tradition began as a part of a Friday night Sabbath meal. Everything about the night was special, even our dress. My three sisters and I wore skirts instead of jeans to the table. We sat in the dining room, and my mother would create one of her memorable dinners.

Most discussions began with one of my parents asking each of us to take a turn answering a specific question: "Do you think the death penalty is wrong?," "Does God exist?," "Should women be drafted?"

In these discussions, we learned to talk about a world larger than our classrooms and to put our thoughts and feelings into words. I remember going to other kids' houses for dinner and being surprised that they didn't talk around the table; *good habits start early.*

Family discussions can be encouraged in a number of ways.

- *With younger kids, read a short story or a riddle that evokes feelings and opinions.*
  Sidney Simon's quizzical, provocative stories in his book *Values Clarification* are a good source.

- *Use topics of school papers as springboards to other topics.*
  A sample topic might be pollution problems, suggested by a science paper.

- *Initiate discussions about various aspects of family life.*
  You might say, "I read a study in the paper today that said kids over the age of ten don't like to stay with baby-sitters. If you were a parent, how would you decide when to leave kids at home alone?"

- *Take a clipping from the newspaper and ask for each person's opinion.*
  Preferably *not* an article about how smoking marijuana leads to permanent hair loss.

- *Read the sports page and follow local teams.*
  Learn the language of sports and how to predict the winner of this year's Super Bowl game.

- *Initiate political conversations.*
  Older kids can form opinions about candidates. Younger ones can answer "political" questions: "If you were elected President, what would be the first thing you would do?"

- *Discuss possibilities for family vacations or weekend activities.*
  Get travel brochures or announcements of special events and let family members express their preferences for your time together.

The success of these discussions depends on your willingness to listen to the thoughts and feelings of family members. You need to share the floor and to allow for opinions very different from your own. Give each person a chance to speak without interruption. Let the younger kids speak first. If the age disparity is too great, let the older kids moderate the discussion or interview their younger brothers or sisters.

Allow room for opinions that don't suit yours: Kids can smell a brainwashing session from miles away. Try to paraphrase each child's viewpoint rather than press your own.

You can start these discussions at any time in the life of your family. Listening to your children's ideas can become a most delightful way of coming to understand each child's special personality.

Kevin, an engineer, talks about the joy of talking and listening to his daughter. "When I get home, I can hang out with Sherry and see what's coming up for her. I can discover what she has learned that day and share her excitement because everything is new."

Listening to your children can help to ease your homecoming, and the enjoyment of your family can be the best reason of all for leaving the office behind.

Part
FIVE

BALANCES

Chapter 12

The Office
at Home

THE PRESIDENT IS HOME

One highly visible office-at-home is the workplace of the President of the United States. And it is widely reported that the advantages and disadvantages of working at home reach the highest office in the land.

Living and working at the White House gave John Kennedy the opportunity to spend more time with his family; he could even see Caroline and John playing from a window in his office. When he wanted to take a break from work, he could step out onto his balcony and talk to them.

This advantage of working at home was offset by interruptions that quickly became media events. Carolyn Sadler recalls these famous interruptions in her book *Children in the White House.*

When former President Truman came to see Kennedy, Caroline was the reception committee, waiting under her father's desk. "How are you?" she inquired. "You used to live here."

John, Jr., once refused to leave a staff meeting. His father decided to ignore him and began the agenda. "What have we got today?" asked Kennedy. "I've got a glass of water," answered his son.

Presidents, along with an estimated ten million other home workers, understand that working at home requires a delicate balance of time at work and at home.

CONVENIENCE/INVASION

All home workers would agree that having an office at home is convenient. Transportation and traffic problems are eliminated. "I have a four-foot commute," noted a consultant with an office across the hall from her bedroom. Ron, a graphic artist, explains, "If I have to work late, I have all of my art supplies right here. I could never cart my materials back and forth from the office."

But the convenience of a home office may be offset by the constant physical presence of your work. Lack of distance from the office can engender a feeling of invasion after work. Helen, a management consultant, explains: "Sometimes I see an octopus leg, crawling out of my office into the living room."

Kelley, a pest control specialist, sees his business phone as the source of the problem. "I can hear the phone ringing even when I am in bed. The other night, a woman called at one o'clock in the morning. She was hysterical because she had just seen a mouse."

The advantage of the physical convenience of your home office contributes to a lack of physical separation from work. Try this technique to make your office a separate territory, one that you can leave behind at the end of the day.

TECHNIQUE: For Business Only

Plan to use your office for the sole purpose of doing business. Don't keep your Universal Gym in the closet. If your office doubles as an exercise room or TV room in the evening, it will be impossible to separate from thoughts about the work.

Just as important, confine your business to your office. Don't spread papers and files all over the house; don't make business calls on the kitchen phone over a cold beer. By all means, establish a separate business line that can be turned off at the end of the workday and transferred to an answering machine or service.

Some home workers say that even if they have an answering machine, they can still hear calls after working hours and are tempted to answer. If you can't resist the sound of a ringing business phone, let an answering service take over for you.

You can enjoy the convenience of an office at home if you can use the office for business only and if you are willing to stay out of the office after work.

FLEXIBILITY/PROCRASTINATION

Having an office at home allows you the flexibility to set your own hours. "Working at home makes it easier to meet weird deadlines," explains Jeanne, a public relations consultant. "I have clients who request projects at the last minute and expect them to be done yesterday."

Karen, who runs a children's clothing retail business from home, enjoys the flexibility of her home-based business. "I'm a night person; when I can't sleep, I come in here and do some sewing."

For many, flexibility leads to procrastination and to the memory of a lesson learned as far back as junior high school: the time needed for any task expands to the amount of time available.

"It is so easy to put things off when the office is right at home," says David, the owner of a party specialty business. "I know I can always do something, the night before, at home."

"Procrastination is habit-forming," notes Jeanne. "It is one thing to be up against a deadline; it's another to get in the habit of letting work expand to fill evenings and weekends."

When you procrastinate, you rob yourself of precious time away from work. Try two techniques to use time wisely and to allow yourself to enjoy the flexibility of working at home, without procrastination.

TECHNIQUE: Office Hours

Alan, a writer noted for witty novels of suspense, plans his time carefully. "I try to keep the same structure as everyone else does. I work Monday through Friday, taking weekends and holidays off. When I want to goof off during working hours, I'll do it in my office. If I decide to read a book, I do it at my desk. I could lie down on the bed, but that would be like being at home."

Plan to set regular working hours. When you work beyond those hours, describe yourself as "working overtime." When you slip into the office after midnight, don't try to kid yourself: it's called moonlighting.

If you struggle to keep your office hours to a reasonable number, you could try to make it more difficult to go to "the office."

TECHNIQUE: Under Lock and Key

For those who can't resist the temptation to slip in and out of the office yet who want to relax after work, a more drastic measure is in order.

Consider the possibility of installing a lock on the door of your office. The more complicated the lock—like a dead bolt—the more inconvenient it will be for you to check into your office for "just a minute."

If you want to extend you working hours, you will have to get out your key, put it in the door and let yourself in. This technique then goes beyond its symbolic function. As you fish for the keys in your pocket, you have time to ask an important question: "Do I really want to work tonight?"

BALANCE/DISTRACTION

Many home workers enjoy the advantages of balancing the demands of work and home. Working at home allows for the possibility of coordinating household maintenance and staying in close contact with young children.

Donna, a data processor, likes the way her business at home helps her to integrate personal and professional time. "It lets me keep an eye on the house. I can do my work and still see that things are running smoothly." Frank is a career counselor who relishes the opportunity to spend extra time with his children. "When I walk out of the office at lunch, the kids say: 'Here's Dad.'"

Working in close proximity to the kitchen and the children can be an attractive advantage for those trying to balance the demands of professional and domestic life. The problem arises when the distractions of working at home overwhelm the time spent working. One home worker admits, "Working at home makes it so easy to take a long leisurely lunch or to go outside and start puttering in the garden. Pretty soon, I am slipping out the door."

Working at home can turn a coffee break into an opportunity to overeat. One computer programmer gained twenty pounds during his first couple of months at home.

The closeness of your children can be a reason for working at home. But children can also provide a continual source of distraction. Matt, a training consultant, describes the interruptions. "I seldom work in long stretches; my three-year-old will come and knock on my door. He'll say, 'Don't work now, Poppa.'"

And Leonard, who operates an accounting service business, echoes the concerns of many home workers about the distractions of friends and neighbors who think that because you are working at home, you are "not really working." "My neighbors know that I work at home so they feel free to come over and interrupt my scheduled day. The other day a neighbor wanted me to help start his car."

To keep yourself from gaining weight or losing your temper, try this next technique practiced by a famous biologist who worked at home.

TECHNIQUE: Darwin's "Sacred Hours"

Charles Darwin's bulletins about the origin of species were issued from the study of a rambling stone house in the village of Down, England. Elbert Hubbard reports in a biography of Darwin that he worked only two hours per day. Darwin's wife and children were aware of his working hours and did not trespass. "Only two hours could I work, and to my wife these hours were sacred. She guarded me as a mother guards her babes."

If you plan to work at home in close proximity to family, friends and neighbors, you will need to find a way to guard your own time. When you work within one hundred feet of the stove, refrigerator and dirty laundry, you must set aside some "sacred time."

Here are some possibilities for protecting more than two hours of your time.

- *Set up definite working hours.*

- *Let friends and neighbors know that you keep definite hours.*
  You can say, "Let me call you back, after work."

- *Get a separate business phone and don't answer your personal phone during your working hours.*
  Put your personal phone on an answering machine or simply unplug it.

- *Label a break as a break.*
  One consultant considers folding towels or loading the dishwasher analagous to a coffee break. If you break for chores, limit the time to fifteen minutes and get back to work.

- *Or don't work on chores during work hours.*
  Another home worker says to her husband, "I'll water the plants *after* I come home from work."

- *Help your children understand your working hours and your need for "sacred," uninterrupted time. Let them know when you will be available to play.*
  Marian, a home-based tutor, explains, "Our children grew up understanding that I had a certain schedule in the morning and that in the afternoon I was available."

- *If necessary, get a baby-sitter during times of intense work deadlines.*

It is important to diminish the distractions so that you can accomplish enough to relax at the end of the day. But sometimes home workers welcome distractions; the interruptions help reduce the isolation of working at home.

PRIVACY/ISOLATION

Richard, a freelance photographer, enjoys the privacy of working at home. "I can do anything I please in my office; I could answer the phone naked if I wanted to. . . ." Other home workers enjoy the psychological comfort of working at home. They can work in jeans or sweats and save money on business attire.

Although the home office has the advantage of privacy, too much privacy can lead to feelings of loneliness and isolation. The factor of isolation is the reason many futurists, including *Megatrends* author John Naisbitt, believe that the utilization of "electronic cottages"—home offices hooked up to corporate computer centers—will never replace the office and the office coffee break. "People seek high-touch environments. The reason people want to go to the office is to be with other people."

One at-home accountant admits to an hour break to watch a soap opera. She conceals her habit from her corporate clients, but finds it an acceptable substitute for the stimulation of office co-workers and the buzz of office gossip.

A consultant who works at home while her husband works at a large engineering firm has difficulty coordinating her needs with her husband's at the end of the day. "When he gets home, he wants to take off his shoes and relax. I want to get to hell out of here!"

To avoid loneliness, cabin fever and television, try the next two techniques. If you can make important contacts during the day, it will be easier to leave work behind.

TECHNIQUE: Connecting with Colleagues

Whatever the nature of your business, there are other people involved in similar work. You can reduce your sense of isolation by connecting with colleagues in your field. Whether you work at home as an accountant, a graphic artist or a management consultant, there are professional associations you can join. The *Encyclopedia of Associations* is available at your public library and lists thousands of possibilities.

Find the organization that most closely matches your business interests. Professionals in specific fields, like accountants or counselors, will find associations more easily. If you run a more specialized business, you might become a member of a network of small-business owners or The National Association of Cottage Industries or one of its local chapters like Northwest Cottage Industries Association. Women's networks with memberships of entrepreneurs and small-business owners can be another rich source of potential associates.

Once you have located an appropriate professional organization, attend meetings regularly with some specific goals in mind.

- Try to cultivate at least five members that you can meet for lunch, coffee or drinks to discuss professional questions and concerns.
- Make a practice of calling newfound associates from time to time for a five-minute professional consultation. Ask for advice, share resources and news.
- If you are genuinely interested, join a planning committee or the board of an organization. This will expand your choice of colleagues.

When you can discuss work concerns with colleagues during the day, you are less likely to spend your evenings consumed by work talk.

TECHNIQUE: Scheduling

As you set up your working goals for the month, plan to schedule time for conversations or meetings with colleagues.

One successful consultant scans her calendar looking for "three or four days of sitting at my desk." She makes sure to schedule lunches or drinks with associates during this time period.

Use your calendar to coordinate a balance of business and

pleasure time. If you see a long stretch of solo work, schedule a movie or play in the evening after work. Call up a friend and invite him or her to dinner.

Allowing yourself time off can be difficult when *you* are the boss. Many people choose to work for themselves in order to enjoy the privilege of being in charge, and many home workers discover themselves to be the toughest boss yet.

MY OWN BOSS/THE TOUGHEST BOSS

The attraction of being in charge is a strong motivation for those people who work at home. They have the opportunity to set goals, salary, working hours and free time. Yet many people who work for themselves are as demanding and difficult as the bosses they left behind. One writer describes himself as "an omniscient boss; I never let myself off the hook."

Home workers who stay "on the hook" have great difficulty leaving work behind and making a transition to more playful activities after work. As a boss, you'll need to treat yourself with care.

TECHNIQUE: The Same Considerations

Learn to treat yourself with the same considerations you would expect to receive if someone *else* was your boss. These considerations include:

- regular working hours
- weekends and holidays off
- vacation time
- recognition and compensation for overtime.

It is essential to recognize the hours that you put into your business. If you can't afford to give yourself a raise, punctuate periods of hard work with other rewards. Recognize the completion of a job and treat yourself to a movie, a novel or an exotic dinner.

Take advantage of being the boss and schedule time off. Ned, a graphic designer, recently bought a horse. He works late into the evenings on Monday through Thursday. At noon on Friday, he takes off to spend the weekend on the ranch where he boards his horse.

Free time and money may be the trading cards. One consultant explains, "Every time I turn down a job, I am turning down money in my pocket. But I value my free time too much to keep myself constantly busy." A data processor uses his initiative as boss to protect his free time. "If I need time to myself, I'll put a client off and ask for more time to complete a project. I'll say, 'I'm booked right now.'"

In the role of boss, be sure to let yourself "go home" at the end of the workday.

COMING HOME FROM WORK

When your office is a "four-foot commute" from home, the difficulties of coming home can be magnified. It is important to practice definite rituals that will allow you to officially enjoy your working day.

TECHNIQUES: A Clean Break

Plan to schedule a break of at least fifteen minutes after you leave your office and before you contend with the logistics of dinner or other plans for the evening.

Karen, a marketing specialist, sees a distinct difference in the days when she takes a break. "I try to take a short break before I pick up the kids. I'll exercise or sit under a sunlamp. When I can do this, things seem smoother with my kids. When I don't take a break, I can be pretty crabby."

The goal is to *leave* the office—even briefly—and return home again. Exercise is ideal for the transition. If time allows, a run, swim or aerobics class will allow for the stimulation of systems sluggish from a day at your desk and will help remove accumulated tensions of the day.

Even household errands can provide a clean break from your office at home. Stopping at the grocery or cleaners can provide an opportunity to gain distance from the day and to practice techniques from earlier chapters.

Remember, as boss, you plan your schedule. If you use time wisely, you can include a break as a daily part of your schedule. Taking a break can be an important "rule of the house."

RULES OF THE HOUSE

By 1990, futurists predict that the number of home workers in America will double. Thirty-five corporations, including Control Data, New York Telephone, Blue Cross and Blue Shield, and Mountain Bell are already experimenting with workers tied into the corporation through a word processor or computer.

Although the desire for person-to-person contact is expected to keep most of America's one hundred million workers in the office, the need for rules of the house to balance and separate work and home will remain the essential challenge of working at home.

Post these rules in your mind:

- Allow for physical separation from your office. Don't use your office for other purposes and be sure to use a separate business phone.
- Keep regular office hours; label working late as "overtime."
- Protect work time from family and domestic distractions. A day of productive work will enable you to leave evenings free.
- Combat isolation by building strong connections with colleagues in your field.
- As a boss, give yourself the same consideration you would receive on any job. Give yourself rewards for outstanding work and time off for good behavior.
- Plan to make a clean break from your office by leaving the house briefly and returning home.

These rules will allow you to maximize the advantages of working at home without denying yourself time to relax and enjoy the people you love.

Chapter 13

Working Together,
Living Together

RACHEL AND HERSCHEL

I n 1912, my grandmother Rachel was sneaking out of her
bedroom window in Babroisk, Russia. She had fallen in love
with a revolutionary. I like to picture her slipping quietly out
of her father's house and running into the forest to meet him.
They would gather with other young Bolsheviks and quietly
enter the soldiers' camps to talk against the violent rule of Czar
Nicholas II.

Rachel's father did not approve of this love and persuaded
Rachel to accept a marriage proposal from Herschel, a distant
cousin in Canada. At seventeen, she traveled from Babroisk to
Montreal to meet Herschel for the first time.

Rachel and Herschel became homesteaders in Selkirk, Man-
itoba. After clearing a rocky piece of land, they built a house and
gardens. Working together, they built a greenhouse, icehouse
and henhouse; all from books that Herschel checked out at the
library.

I remember the way Rachel described her years of working

with Herschel: with her Bette Davis eyes shining, she would say, "I always pulled the wagon."

My grandparents were a loving couple, typical of those who worked together in the early 1900s. Work was the centerpiece of their lives, and little thought was given to the pursuit of leisure or the idea of separating work and home.

Here are seven contemporary couples who struggle with the pleasures and frustrations of sharing a professional life together. Each illuminates an essential area of balance for couples who live and work together.

David and Sandra:
"We Carve Out Our Turf"

David and Sandra met in the research lab where they now work as a team. He is a vascular surgeon; she is a biologist. Together, they are exploring the process of the disease arteriosclerosis, working with animal subjects in a hospital laboratory.

Sandra credits their mutual interest in other things and their ability to "carve out our own turf" as the basis for this relationship of work and love. She says these distinctions keep her in the lab and away from thoughts about "selling flowers on a street corner."

Sandra and David have a clear-cut division of labor in their research: He is responsible for generating the experimental design of the research; she runs the lab and carries out the experiments.

The importance of separate responsibilities for each member of a working couple cannot be overestimated. Still, many couples seek togetherness at all levels of a joint project. Instead, they find conflict and confusion and can carry those feelings home with them. A clear definition of roles serves two purposes: Each partner has an arena of personal power, and each can experience a definite sense of accomplishment within that arena.

If you and your partner have been working without the clarity of role descriptions, try this next technique to put your responsibilities into words.

TECHNIQUE: **Writing the Want Ads**

In a relaxed atmosphere, sit down with your partner, bring paper and pen and set up the following hypothetical situation.

You have decided to let two other people run your business while you take a sabbatical in the south of France. Write two separate want ads for the Sunday paper. The first ad should describe the responsibilities of your position. The second should describe the responsibilities of your partner's position.

Take at least fifteen minutes to carefully describe each of your positions. Then trade written ads and compare the points of similarity and differences.

The ads can launch a process of role negotiation. Don't end the discussion until each of you has written your "new" job description. Sometimes role definitions are related to a shared set of plans about the future of your joint venture.

Janet and Jeffrey:
"Planning Is the Hardest Thing"

Janet and Jeffrey are partners in a twenty-year marriage and a ten-year business venture that has grown to include four highly successful hair and beauty care centers. They have been careful to divide job responsibilities and stand behind each other's on-the-job decisions.

They both have found planning to be the hardest part of running the business. "We have set financial goals and shared common thoughts; we read, research and talk to other hair stylists. Most important, we need to know what each of our commitments will be."

Every family business venture needs to operate with a clear sense of present responsibilities and future goals. Ideas about the future that remain unspoken can compromise the sense of a shared vision. Day-to-day business decisions are often based on your own inner image of what the future holds. Take time to confirm that you and your partner are heading toward the same future.

Try the next technique to explore the future plans of your shared partnership.

Take a moment and speculate about some future scenarios. Each of you can jot down the answer to three questions:

- In two years what will our top work priorities be?
- In five years, what do I see myself/you doing?
- What will our business/work be like in ten years?

Compare your answers and use the conversation to stimulate talk about your shared future. Welcome differences of opinion as opportunities to refine a shared sense of purpose.

The next couple suggests that learning to resolve differences in the *present* is the top survival skill for working partnerships.

Julie and Alan: *"The Sense of Impending Doom"*

Julie and Alan are the owners of a video production company that offers clients services ranging from rental to full-scale commercial production work. They enjoy a volatile, creative relationship at work, balanced by a broad range of independent leisure activities.

Julie acknowledges their differences with a sense of humor: "Sometimes during a shoot, we get really mad at each other. We stand there so tight-jawed we can't even speak; but we still have to continue working and present a professional image. We try to deal with conflicts *immediately* after the incident. I don't want to live with a sense of impending doom, that he's just about to bring something up."

The resolution of differences, whether they relate to roles or to future day-to-day frustrations, is *the* critical factor that determines whether working partners can "come home" from work at the end of the day.

Unlike the boss or colleagues you leave behind at the office, our angry spouse and unresolved tensions accompany you ome and can spoil your evening. Practice the careful art of criticism to initiate the process of resolving work problems *on the job.*

TECHNIQUE: Not the Kitchen Sink

Working partners need to be able to criticize each other with a delicate but definite touch. The strongest temptation is to generalize about your partner's behavior. Each partner knows the other's annoying habits at work and at home. When one criticizes, he or she tends literally to bring in the kitchen sink.

Suppose that you have been frustrated with your partner's inability to organize his desk. Instead of limiting the criticism to the desk, you may add some domestic data for extra punch: "It reminds me of the way you leave your dirty ashtrays in the kitchen sink!"

Effective criticism between professionals should be limited to the job itself. Limit your criticism to the *exact behavior* that is bothering you. Follow three steps:

- *State the exact behavior of your concern; include time, place and frequency of behavior.*
  Example: "This morning I needed to consult yesterday's sales journal and you hadn't recorded the numbers."

- *State your viewpoint and explain how the behavior affected you.*
  Example: "I got really frustrated because I needed the information for an inventory and I had to postpone it until you finished."

- *Suggest a plan for change. Tell the other person that you want him or her to start or stop acting in a particular way.*
  Example: "I think we can avoid this problem if you would be willing to complete the journal at the end of each day. If you don't have time, let me know before we leave."

The key to offering criticism between intimates is to keep focused on the specifics of the behavior and to agree on a plan for change. This kind of criticism is easier for the listener to absorb. If your partner hasn't mastered the art of specific criticism, you can become skilled in listening to criticism about your work.

TECHNIQUE: The Best Defense

You may react to criticism with an immediate defense. If he or she tells you that you "always" get impatient with customers, you will think of a time when you displayed saintly perseverance.

In an earlier chapter, I mentioned that you can listen two to three times faster than someone else can talk. Most people use that time to prepare their defense against the criticism. But why not use the time to *understand* your partner's concerns?

You time together will be undermined until you are willing to consider the criticism. Remember three guidelines in clarifying criticism:

- *After your partner's initial critical statement, ask a series of questions that will help you to clarify and paraphrase his or her concerns.*
  If she makes a general statement, invite him or her to be more specific. *Example*:

YOUR PARTNER: You are so disorganized.
YOU: Do you mean my desk or my files?
PARTNER: Your files. I have trouble finding client receipts.

- *Ask yourself a series of questions to clarify the validity of the criticism.*
  Examples: Have I noticed this? Have I heard this before at another job?

- *Clarify possible plans for changing your behavior; find out what your partner has in mind.*
  Example:

YOU: Do you have a filing system in mind?
PARTNER: Yes, I'd like you to file orders using the client name, rather than the date received.

The effective use of criticism can dissolve feelings of unfinished business between partners. But don't forget to add praise to your resolution of the day. Be specific about how your partner made a strong creative contribution to your working relationship.

The techniques of gentle, pointed criticism and deliberate praise can become a part of your rituals in ending the day. Try to resolve the conflicts before you leave work or before settling into an evening at home.

Margaret and Ted:
"We Mark the End of the Day"

Margaret and Ted jointly operate a personal development service which offers vocational and personal counseling, as well as educational tutoring and testing. They both work at home with strict rules about separating professional and personal time.

Margaret explains, "We both work from 8:00 to 5:00, and we have a definite way to mark the end of the day. At 5:00, we clean up the office, turn on the answering machine and that's *it*." Because they work at home, Margaret and Ted are careful to keep their office at a distance. After 5:00 o'clock they do not use the office space for any personal business.

Working partners need to create homecoming rituals that mark the end of the working day and the beginning of a relaxed and playful evening together. You may choose to create debriefing activities as a couple and as individuals.

The most essential shared ritual of closure for working partners is the resolution of differences. The techniques in the previous section can decrease the likelihood of a hard day's night.

An interval of time apart can be an important chance to create a transition between work and home.

TECHNIQUE: A Separate Peace

Couples who work together don't always share the same experiences. With a clear division of labor, each person may have a separate set of experiences to review; each needs time to release accumulated tensions of the day.

Try to arrange some individual time on your way home from work. Give yourself the opportunity to indulge in fantasies of revenge and glory; take time to express anger about difficult customers or to bask in your sense of accomplishment.

Use your private time to exercise or to experiment with some of the techniques listed in earlier chapters. Attend a meeting of your pet political action group, have a drink with a friend or colleague, sit in the sauna.

Time away from your partner will allow you to meet at home, refreshed and at peace with your feelings about work.

Sometimes even the most carefully planned transitions make

it difficult to keep from spending the evening absorbed in talk about work.

Karen and Doug:
"We Say, Stop Work"

Karen and Doug started their balloon delivery service one summer, with a helium tank in their second bedroom. Several years later, they were operating out of an 800-square-foot office space with a small fleet of delivery vans. They clearly enjoy each other's company "on a number of levels," yet both find it tempting to slip into conversations about work during evening and weekend hours.

"We'll be eating a lazy Sunday breakfast," says Karen, "and suddenly one of us will have an idea for the business. If it's me, Doug will say, 'We'll discuss it tomorrow.'"

Working partners need definite techniques to postpone thoughts and talk about their shared business. Try two techniques to prevent your time at home from being consumed by a business agenda.

TECHNIQUE: Thought Stopping à Deux

In the first chapter, I described the technique of thought stopping and how it might have relieved Lady Macbeth's thoughts (see page 25). Working partners can help each other control the intrusion of thoughts about work.

Doug and Karen have established code phrases to turn off work talk. Doug elaborates, "Whenever I bring up a new idea or an old problem, Karen will say: 'Uh-uh, not now' or 'Relax.' I even made a sign and posted it over the kitchen sink. It says, *STOP WORK*."

The most difficult thoughts to stop are shiny, new ideas. Most partners are convinced that if they don't talk about the idea immediately they will lose their train of thought.

TECHNIQUE: Catching the Next Train

You are sitting in Symphony Hall, enjoying a romantic Brahms violin concerto. Suddenly you have a brilliant idea for promoting your Christmas sale. You furtively open your program, squinting to visualize the perfect advertising copy.

During intermission your wife frowns and asks, "Why were you staring at your program?" Your answer: "I had a great idea for our Christmas promotion and I didn't want to lose my train of thought."

A new idea can present itself with an urgency that demands to be heard and threatens to evaporate. It is important to remember that many good ideas will occur more than once, and that your memory can be coaxed into recollection.

Next time you try to chase a train of thought, do one of two things:

- Jot down a one-sentence reminder to yourself on a matchbook, cocktail napkin or shirt sleeve.
- Tell your partner, "Remind me to tell you about my idea for our December sale. The idea is to use penguins; remind me about penguins."

With practice, you can become skilled at training your memory to catch the next train.

Laura and Mack: "Take Time to Enjoy"

Laura and Mack are owners of a small retail clothing store. Their seasonal trips to New York, Milan and Paris fill the store with elegant ready-to-wear apparel. They make a special effort to "beam out work" and put a high premium on shared activities and sunny vacations. Laura says, "We both work hard and give it our all. If we don't take time to enjoy the lifestyle we have earned, what's the point? We try very hard to look at our life as a whole."

Working partners, like Mack and Laura, can set goals for leisure as well as for work (see Chapter 9). These goals are a deliberate reminder of one of the reasons for working hard: to enjoy the luxury of time off.

A lack of interests beyond work can lead to repetitive conversations. Couples whose lives are centered in work gravitate to shoptalk out of boredom, inertia or a fear of silence.

Partners need to plan for afterwork activities that are vital, stimulating and rewarding.

TECHNIQUE: The Whole Picture

Take the opportunity to discuss the balance of work and leisure time with your partner. Using the Leisure Survey in chapter 9 (see page 141), ask each other a series of key questions:

- Are you satisfied with the amount of time we spend on mutual leisure activity?
- Are you satisfied with the amount of time we spend in individual leisure pursuits?
- Are we enjoying our choices on weekends and vacations?
- When is the last time we tried a new activity?

Make a practice of looking at the whole picture of your life together. Use discontent as an opportunity to consider new possibilities.

Naomi and Jeff: *"It's an Incredible Connection"*

Naomi and Jeff are the owners of a busy urban delicatessen. Famous for its borscht and sour cream coffee cake, the restaurant turns into a music club during the evenings. Naomi manages the books, and Jeff handles the booking of musical acts. Both guard against letting the restaurant "devour our lives."

Naomi speaks for many working partners when she describes the balance of difficulty and delight in her partnership with Jeff. "The restaurant is like a child, it's an incredible connection. We know that we love each other and that conflict is inevitable. Our mutual joy gets us through the hard times."

By practicing techniques to achieve a separation of work and home, each couple can experience the special joy of working together and living together.

Chapter 14

Coming Home Alone

THREE SINGLE SOLUTIONS

The challenge of coming home alone lies in feeling comfortable being alone while at the same time being eager to open up your home to the joys of friendship and romance. Consider three familar patterns that blur the distinctions between work and home. Each offers an incomplete solution to the experience of living alone.

Home Away from Home

In the year following her divorce, Terry, a financial adviser, found the thought of going home to her empty house unbearable. She began to work late and soon discovered that a number of her colleagues also worked into the evening.

Within a month, Terry had a new pattern: working late and afterward joining other overtimers for a drink or snack. She would get home just in time to get ready for bed.

"These people are like a second family to me," she said.

The Empty Calendar

Holly is a family physican with a busy, growing practice. She is at the hospital at 7:00 A.M. for rounds and in her office by 8:00, often scheduling patients until 7:00 at night.

She frequently makes and cancels plans to meet friends for dinner or a concert. "I can never tell what kind of day it will be. Sometimes the prospect of a planned evening becomes very unattractive."

The Empty House

David is an attorney who has lived alone since he graduated from college ten years ago. In fact, he is still living in the same apartment, with the same secondhand furniture.

After work, he moves at an Olympian pace: tennis, season tickets to the theater, symphony and basketball games. He serves on the board of directors of two arts organizations and is co-chairman of this year's United Way campaign. David laughs and admits, "I haven't eaten a meal at home since 1980."

These three solutions can't offer the balance of a comfortable home and a connection with people just outside the door. Take a closer look at each solution.

Solution #1:
Home Away from Home

Following her divorce, Terry learned that the single lifestyle creates opportunities for working overtime. She drew a very thin line to separate her life at work and at home.

Refugees from divorce and from the unpredictable prospects of dating often turn to work as a soothing source of self-esteem. One accountant explains, "When my relationships with men fizzle, I find it easy to get involved in work. When I work hard, I get money, praise and a definite sense of accomplishment."

Spending extra time at work enables many singles to spend the majority of their time involved in something that gives them a sense of power and control.

If you work late, you can be sure you will finish writing your project summary. If you go to a party, you may meet the same old cast of undesirables.

In these ways, working late becomes a predictable, if limited, world to inhabit. In time, work colleagues become stand-ins for genuine loving friendships.

You need to guard against Terry's solution of overwork to compensate for an empty life after work. Do you recognize any of these signs?

- A head count of your friends reveals that they all work in your office or in your field.
- You can easily postpone work tasks for evenings and weekends.
- Your only birthday card last year was from the office support staff.
- You spend at least three evenings a week with professional organizations.

Try the next technique to expand your circle of friends and increase the possibilities of a rich life after work.

TECHNIQUE: The Whole Galaxy

Fans of Gene Roddenberry's *Star Trek* will remember that Captain Kirk, Dr. McCoy and Mr. Spock of the starship *Enterprise* had no home. During their "five-year mission to explore other worlds," all crew members worked and lived aboard the starship.

Their friendships were limited to each other and to the strange assortment of people who were "beamed up" by Scotty's transporter. No wonder the men always fell in love with such bizarre and unsuitable women, like the women whose tears enslaved Captain Kirk, or the alien who tried to steal Spock's brain.

I am not saying that you can't meet charming people at work; but I am suggesting that there is a whole galaxy of possibilities if you are willing to look outside of your office.

Make a deliberate attempt to broaden your circle of friends. Using the Leisure Survey in Chapter 9, identify at least two areas of interest and pleasure. Next, find and join an organization or club for people of similar interests.

Forget about bars and getting on the guest list for Truman Capote's masked ball. Find people who share a common interest with you. Whether you volunteer to help out a museum or get involved with a political campaign, begin to fill in your social calendar after work.

Solution #2:
The Empty Calendar

Like Dr. Holly, many working professionals often make and then cancel plans for the hours after work. Their calendars are overbooked during the day, and their evenings and weekends are completely free. Holly's scheduling points to the strongest advantage and the clearest disadvantage of coming home alone.

When you first arrive at home, you have the opportunity to unwind without meeting the emotional demands of a partner or children. You can enjoy the luxury of a three-hour bubble bath, taking time to cast off your fears about work and to scheme about the future.

You can enjoy a leisurely dinner, thinking about the frustrating people in your day and making plans to finish projects tomorrow. The problem arises when your time to unwind extends into the entire evening or weekend.

Without the interruptions of a friend or family member, your preoccupation with work can continue until you go to sleep. This aspect of living alone can result in constant thoughts about work.

Your empty calendar is the beginning of a life pattern of self-absorption. Do these signs sound familiar?

- You have changed plans at the last minute twice this month.
- You haven't seen a movie since *E.T.*

- Your friends introduce plans with the proviso, "You can always change your mind."
- Your daytime appointments are written in ink, evenings in pencil.

Each time you decline to join a friend or lover, you reinforce the idea that you cannot manage a life that includes both work and love. Instead of convincing yourself, try two techniques that cultivate the habit of carrying out plans after work.

TECHNIQUE: Reconnect

Before you reach for the phone to cancel dinner with a friend, think back to the good feelings that prompted you to want to spend time with him or her.

Greg, a management consultant, describes the situation: "Sometimes at the end of the day I feel too tired or wound up to get together with friends. But, instead of cancelling, I let myself remember our last visit. Then I can reconnect with the good feelings I had when we made the plans."

When you can reconnect with positive feelings, your plans for the evening may become appealing. If your imagination doesn't make the connection, pick up the telephone.

TECHNIQUE: Confirm

In the midst of a busy week, you may approach dinner with a friend as if it were another item on your "to do" list. If you begin to confuse professional and personal time, call your friend to confirm your dinner together. In many cases, just the sound of your friend's voice will stimulate your memories of good times together and help you to honor your plans to meet.

"I can't count the number of times I have called to cancel drinks," said one broker. "But when I call, I hear a friend's voice and suddenly I *want* to get together."

For other people, staying at home is the act that takes a deliberate effort.

Solution #3:
The Empty House

David, the attorney, is like a painter living through his "orange period"—orange crate, that is. Even with his substantial income, he has never invested in furniture or dishes, has not even bought a comfortable chair for his living room. His home is a combination of a bus stop and storage locker.

The emptiness and discomfort of his home became a good excuse for spending every evening away and coming home only to sleep or to change clothes.

David's empty house and full social calendar is only a partial solution to the challenge of living alone. Do you recognize any of these signs?

- You always meet friends; no one ever picks you up "at home."
- You don't have even *one* of these things: garlic press, pot holder, recipe.
- You have had the same travel poster on your wall since the 1968 World's Fair.
- You find it difficult to spend money on anything for your home.

You need to learn to feel comfortable in the silence and serenity of your own home. If you are uncomfortable spending time at home, you rob yourself of precious time to relax and recuperate from work.

TECHNIQUE: Home Investment

Stop thinking of your home as a place to change clothes after work. If you want to create a life separate from your work, you need to invest in your home.

Investment means time and money. You don't need expensive furniture; get involved in the process of creating a home that is a reflection of your personality and your own needs for comfort and beauty.

You don't have to be a designer to find a couch or chair that would be a great spot to read the paper, or to buy a painting that reminds you of your favorite beach in California. Look in furniture stores and magazines for inspiration, and learn to trust your own instincts. You are not redecorating for a photo layout for *Architectural Digest*; you are trying to create a living room that will entice *you* to come home and put your feet up.

Many singles refrain from investing in their homes because they fear making a "commitment" to a single lifestyle. Remember that your situation can change at any time.

Bernice decided to borrow money to invest in furniture for her apartment. She bought an elegant sleeper sofa and a striking Oriental rug. Two months later she met and married a wonderful man and spent the rest of the money on their new home. The sleeper is in their spare bedroom.

Think about the possibility of buying a house or condominium. Owning a condo will not keep you from marrying, but it will reduce your income taxes and increase your joint assets if you do marry.

Now that you have a place to sit down, what's for dinner?

TECHNIQUE: Home on the Range

You'll feel more comfortable coming home if you can prepare some simple dishes for yourself. Buy a cookbook of recipes for one, or learn to identify which takeout places have food that lends itself to reheating.

Make dinner at home a pleasant ritual. If you treat yourself to colorful dinner plates, you won't eat out of plastic containers. Put on your favorite music and eat slowly.

Even if you can't cook, if you are familiar with the items at a delicatessen or bakery, you are ready to invite friends into your home.

TECHNIQUE: Open House

Inviting friends and lovers into your home is a delightful way of learning to feel comfortable spending time at home. You don't need to plan a dinner party; begin with simple invitations.

Extend an invitation for coffee and dessert, organize a potluck dinner or offer wine and cheese before a concert or play.

As host, you will cultivate a sense of pride and comfort in your home. As you attend to the needs of your guests and try to help them feel at home, you will find that you suddenly feel the same way.

Epilogue

You Can Go Home Again

S everal months ago I presented a talk to a group of travel industry executives. Afterward, a woman rushed up to me and said, "I am going straight home to apologize to my husband. I have been carrying on about work for weeks!"

As she left the meeting, she was planning to return home with some new beliefs and some practical ideas about how to make those beliefs come alive in her life with her husband.

As you have read these pages, I hope that you have accepted the challenge of leaving your office behind and that at least five of the techniques will become a permanent part of your homecoming.

I hope, too, that you have been persuaded to discard the "three cherished but dangerous beliefs" about coming home, and to consider some compelling alternatives.

BELIEF #1:
"MY FAMILY AND FRIENDS WILL UNDERSTAND"

I read an interview recently in which a local celebrity offered a variation on his belief: "My family knows they come first," he said emphatically. But later in the interview, he admitted to "a tendency to be a workaholic. . . ."

You can't expect your family to understand that they come first if you indulge your tendency to work overtime or come home with a briefcase full of unfinished business.

I have tried to emphasize the idea that you *can't* have it all. You simply can't be in two places at one time, nor can you be in two different states of mind. You can't work weekends *and* coach your daughter's softball team. You can't be simultaneously thinking about work *and* responding to the emotional needs of your family and friends.

What you want your family and friends to understand is that you value a clear distinction between your private life and your business life and that you are willing to practice techniques that allow you to leave unfinished business at your office.

Alternative belief: "My family and friends understand that our time together after work needs to be protected from my pressures at work."

BELIEF #2:
"AT HOME, I CAN REALLY BE MYSELF"

When a solicitor for a charitable organization comes calling at home, we often say: "I gave at the office." In a more general sense, we often "give" both money and our very best behavior at the office.

A thoughtful woman who typed an early draft of this book confessed that she had an identity crisis while reading as she typed. "Who am I really?" she asked me. "Am I the thoughtful person I am at the office, or the grouchy person I am at home?"

Help yourself to the techniques that allow you to express your attentive, loving and empathic self after work. This version of "being yourself" gives expression to your capacity for generosity, humor and sensuality.

Alternative belief: "At home, I have an opportunity to show a vulnerable, responsive side of myself."

BELIEF #3:
"THIS IS ONLY TEMPORARY"

Some difficult situations really *are* temporary. George Washington reportedly slept only three hours a night during the Revolutionary War. This is very different from sleepwalking through months and months of a stressful work situation.

Valerie took a job as a magazine editor before her contract as a radio talk-show host had expired. For three months she was getting up at 5 A.M. to be on the air and then spending eight hours on the magazine.

"During the first weeks, I had to keep reminding myself: This crunch is only temporary, but I know the damage to my relationship with Virgil and the kids could last much longer."

During the "temporary" hard times, like a new job or a project deadline, you need to step up your commitment to using transitional techniques. You should also remember that temporary times can stretch into years.

Alternative belief: "My situation at work may be temporary, but the effects of my behavior will last for a long time."

You can go home again. Armed with new beliefs and techniques to put them into daily practice, you'll be ready for the journey home.

Bon voyage.